The Multiple-Dog Family

SHEILA WEBSTER BONEHAM, Ph.D.

The Multiple-Dog Family
Project Team
Editors: Craig Sernotti, Stephanie Fornino
Copy Editor: Stephanie Fornino
Indexer: Joann Woy
Design concept: Leah Lococo Ltd., Stephanie Krautheim
Design layout: Stephanie Krautheim

T.F.H. Publications
President/CEO: Glen S. Axelrod
Executive Vice President: Mark E. Johnson
Publisher: Christopher T. Reggio
Production Manager: Kathy Bontz

T.F.H. Publications, Inc.
One TFH Plaza
Third and Union Avenues
Neptune City, NJ 07753

*Discovery Communications, LLC Book
Development Team:*
Marjorie Kaplan, President and General Manager,
Animal Planet Media
Patrick Gates, President, Discovery Commerce
Elizabeth Bakacs, Vice President, Creative and
Merchandising
Sue Perez-Jackson, Director, Licensing
Bridget Stoyko, Designer

09 10 11 12 1 3 5 7 9 8 6 4 2
Printed and bound in Indonesia
Library of Congress Cataloging-in-Publication Data

Boneham, Sheila Webster, 1952
  The multiple-dog family / Sheila Webster Boneham.
     p. cm. – (Animal planet pet care library)
  Includes index
  ISBN 978-0-7938-3704-5 (alk. paper)
  1. Dogs. I. Title.
  SF427.B62 2009
  636.7–dc22
                        2008046832

This book has been published with the intent to provide accurate and authoritative information in regard
to the subject matter within. While every reasonable precaution has been taken in preparation of this book,
the author and publisher expressly disclaim responsibility for any errors, omissions, or adverse effects aris-
ing from the use or application of the information contained herein. The techniques and suggestions are
used at the reader's discretion and are not to be considered a substitute for veterinary care. If you suspect a
medical problem consult your veterinarian.

The Leader in Responsible Animal Care for Over 50 Years!™

www.tfhpublications.com

Table of Contents

Chapter 1

The

Domestic Pack

Big and small, fluffy and sleek, rambunctious and dignified, quiet and loud, a rainbow of colors and a plethora of personalities—enter the wonderfully diverse world of domestic dogs. With so much to choose from, no wonder approximately half of the nearly 36 million US households that have a dog own more than one.

Perhaps you already live with two or more dogs. Or maybe you're thinking of adding a second, or third, dog to your family, or of going from zero to two in one adoption. Whatever your multiple-dog status, there's something in this book for you. My goal is to help make living with more than one dog easier for you and your dogs so that you can focus on the good stuff.

The Pleasure of Their Company

We could fill this entire book with reasons for having more than one dog. If you're gone from home for long hours, your dogs have the companionship of each other. If your dog is getting on in years, he may be rejuvenated by a younger canine playmate, and you may feel less apprehensive about your older dog's advancing age. Besides, dogs give us so much love and are so much fun that it's often hard to resist the urge to have just one more.

If you already own more than one dog and have no plans to add to your canine family, you may simply be looking for ways to make your current pack run more smoothly. Keep reading—there's information here on everything from safe homes and safe travel to nutrition, health care, training, and behavior management.

If you're thinking of adding a second (or third, or...) dog to your family, this book will help you plan ahead for smooth introductions and harmonious long-term relationships.

Do You Really Want More Than One?

Before you expand your canine family, there are some things you need to consider. Let's take a look.

If one dog gives so much love, more than one dog gives even more.

Costs

Responsible care costs money. The more dogs you have, the more money you have to spend to take proper care of them. Each of your dogs needs nutritious food (see Chapter 4) and regular veterinary care. (See Chapter 7.) Some breeds require regular grooming and trimming (see Chapter 5), which cost time, money, or both. You'll need some basic equipment—collars, leashes, crates, beds, toys, treats, and so on. (See Chapter 3.) Many communities require you to purchase a license for each of your dogs (more on this in a moment). Although some supplies for smaller dogs cost a bit less, responsible care for any dog carries a cost.

Time

More dogs also require more of your time. If you want a peaceable kingdom, you must give each of your dogs at least basic obedience training (see Chapter 6), and they all need daily exercise. Dogs create the need for more housecleaning, some more than others, and with more than one dog you'll have more bowls to clean, more bedding to wash, and more vacuuming and floor washing to do. The more dogs you have, the more poop you'll scoop. And every one of your dogs needs and deserves some individual attention every single day.

Restrictions

Some communities have passed legal limits on the number of dogs a person may own (more on this in a moment), so before you add another pooch to

SENIOR DOG TIP

Old Dogs and Young

Older dogs often seem rejuvenated by the addition of a puppy or younger adult to the family. However, the old guys are sometimes overwhelmed by puppies and adolescents who want to play, and play rough, much of the time. If you have one or more elderly dogs who can no longer take rough play, plan ahead before you add a young dog to the family. Provide a refuge for your senior away from ear pulling and body slamming. Teach the newcomer some manners, and spend some private time with your old friend. Let the dogs interact as long as the oldster is comfortable, but don't let a roughneck pup (or adult) overwhelm his elder.

7

your porch, be sure that your dogs will all be legal. Fines for violations are often substantial, and you may be forced give up one or more of your pets.

Your insurance company may have something to say about your decision to get another dog, or your choice of dogs, as well. Whether we like it or not, some breeds are blacklisted—not only legally in some places but also by insurance companies that consider them to be too risky. The breeds included on some of these lists would probably surprise you. In any case, you may want to check your coverage with your insurance agent before you acquire another dog or before you choose a breed.

How Many Are too Many?

I've heard it said that you can't have too many dogs. In terms of sheer love that may be true, but practically, it's a dangerous idea. We can have too many dogs, and when people do, the dogs are the big losers.

How many are too many? That depends on you (and the legal climate where you live). For some people at some stages of life, one dog is too many. Other people can manage two, or five, or more. Here are a few questions to consider as you think about how many dogs you should have.

How Many Can You Afford?

Besides the everyday cost of routine care, you should plan for unusual expenses. What if one of your dogs broke a leg or required emergency surgery? What if two or more of them became seriously ill at the

same time? As dogs age, their medical expenses often increase, so you need to plan for that as well.

Do You Have the Time?

Although their individual needs will vary, every single dog needs exercise, training, and personal attention every single day, without fail, no matter what else is happening in your life and family. Every dog also needs regular grooming and at least basic obedience training.

How Many Can You Accommodate?

This isn't just a matter of size but also of activity, noise, and cleanliness. More are not merrier if they don't have room to run and play safely, or if their barking drives the neighbors mad, or if you can't keep the poop picked up.

Be certain that you can afford more than one dog, as well as devote time to each of your furry friends.

FAMILY-FRIENDLY TIP

Safety for Kids and Dogs

Kids and dogs can be the best of friends, but they do have to learn how to interact safely and kindly with one another. A tragic number of children are bitten every year, usually by their own family dogs or dogs they know. Most bites can be prevented. Here's how you can do your part:

- Teach your dogs and any children with whom they interact to treat one other gently and with respect.

- See that all of your dogs have basic obedience training, and keep reinforcing that training.

- Socialize your dogs thoroughly, especially with children.

- Have your dogs altered (spayed or neutered)—both male and female dogs are less likely to bite when their urge to reproduce is removed.

- Supervise all interactions between young dogs and young children, and be ready to intervene immediately.

- With older children and dogs, use good judgment based on the individuals, not their ages. Err on the side of caution.

- Dogs almost never bite without warning, but people—especially children—often miss the warning. Learn to read your dogs, take any warning behavior seriously, and don't allow children to push your dogs beyond their tolerance.

- Discourage rough play, especially with more than one dog and child involved—things can get out of hand in a heartbeat.

- Teach your child not to tease dogs; pretend to bark or growl at dogs; stare at a dog; try to take things away from a dog; disturb a dog who is sleeping, eating, ill or injured, or caring for puppies. Don't allow anyone of any age to tease your dogs.

- Teach children never to approach a strange dog without the owner's permission, to approach all dogs slowly and quietly, and to let the dog sniff their hands before petting

Could You Evacuate Everyone in an Emergency?

A friend who lost her home to wildfires a few years ago raised a question on an Internet discussion list that's worth considering: If you had to evacuate, could you take all of your household pets as well as your human family with you? If not, you have too many.

Legal Issues

Most municipalities have laws affecting pet owners and ownership, and every year more laws are passed. Some of these so-called dog laws benefit responsible pet owners and their neighbors alike. Others infringe on your right to share your life with dogs and other domestic animals without providing any real benefit to anyone.

Some existing and proposed laws sound good on the surface but aren't good if you look closely. To protect your rights as a dog owner, know your local laws and keep track of proposed laws. Your local animal control or city or county government office should be able to give you a copy of the legal code applying to animals where you live. Local kennel clubs, breed clubs, training clubs, and the Internet can provide information on the implications of proposed and existing legislation that may hurt you and your dogs. Know where political candidates stand on pet laws, and vote to protect your dogs and your rights.

Now let's look at a few of the more common types of laws affecting dogs and their people.

Licensing

Your state and local laws probably require you to license your dogs. Proof of rabies vaccination is usually required, so one argument for dog licensing is that it cuts down on the spread of this terrible disease, reducing the risk of exposure for people. Other arguments are that licensing reduces pet overpopulation and promotes responsible ownership. In reality, people who comply with the licensing laws are already responsible dog owners, and those who see licensing as government intrusion and an unnecessary expense often simply don't license their dogs.

Regardless of how you view the politics of licensing, it may offer some benefits. A license tag on a lost dog's collar generally improves the chances that he'll be returned to his owner and may even save his life where available shelter space is limited and animals without tags are euthanized quickly. And of course, licensing your dogs puts you in compliance with the law.

The cost for dog licenses varies widely from place to place and may depend on the owner's age (seniors sometimes get discounts), whether the animals are altered (spayed or neutered), and other factors. Check with your veterinarian or local authorities for more on licenses.

Numbers Limits

Many communities now limit the number of dogs and other pets a person can own legally. Supporters of limit laws claim that the limits prevent pets from becoming nuisances, but that claim doesn't hold up under scrutiny. The problem isn't multiple pets but irresponsible owners. One dog barking all day, running loose, pottying in the neighbors' yards, and bothering people and other animals is more trouble for the community than several dogs who are properly confined and controlled. If you're a responsible owner, your pets are never a nuisance or a danger to your neighbors.

Limits on pet ownership are difficult to enforce, and they don't solve the problem of irresponsible ownership. In fact, laws limiting pet ownership solely on the basis of numbers have been successfully challenged around the country, but there have also been many sad

The law may limit the number of dogs you're allowed to own. Check with your local municipality to find out if laws exist.

PACK TIP

The Upside and Downside of More Than One Dog

Living with two or more dogs can be wonderful. If they get along, you'll have a window into the emotional and behavioral world of another species. Your dogs will have one another for play, for company, and for cuddles and kisses. And of course, you will have one more canine to love and to love you. But before you add another dog to your home pack, it's important to be aware of the downside of having more than one. Each of your dogs needs individual attention, training, and grooming. If their physical needs are different, you'll have to spend more time giving them individualized exercise. You'll also spend more money on food, veterinary care, equipment, toys, training classes, boarding, and other "things for dogs."

cases of people having to give up one or more of their dogs because they had, say, four dogs instead of the legal three.

You may think that numbers limits don't affect you because you only have two or three dogs. Please think again. Limits are arbitrary, and if the limit can be set at five today, tomorrow it may be lowered to two. Or one. Or none. It makes more sense for communities to enforce existing nuisance and confinement laws than to pass new, arbitrary laws that penalize responsible pet owners and do nothing to address the real issues.

Dog Safety

Whether or not it's legal where you live, if your dogs run loose, they are in danger. They may be hit by motor vehicles, stolen, poisoned, shot, injured or killed by other animals, or subjected to cruelty by people. Loose dogs can also be a serious nuisance and potentially dangerous to livestock, pets, and people, especially if they join together. Dogs in packs are like people in mobs—they lose their individual inhibitions and do things they wouldn't normally do, things you might never expect of your pets. Even those of us who own and love dogs don't want your dog digging up our zinnias, pooping in our yards, or harassing our pets.

Fence Your Yard

The best way to keep your dogs home is with a secure fence. It should be high enough to prevent your best jumper from leaping over and snug enough to the ground to keep your smallest pooch from wriggling or digging under. Gates should have secure latches. If you can't afford to fence your entire yard, why not enclose an area large enough for your dogs to potty and get a little exercise and fresh air?

Chains Are for Tires, not Dogs

Chaining or tying dogs outside and leaving them there is highly inappropriate and often cruel. Chains and ropes can wrap around a dog's body and cause serious, even life-threatening injuries. They can wrap around trees and other objects until the dog is unable to move. A dog on a chain or rope is vulnerable to teasing, attack, or theft, or to breaking loose and becoming lost. Some jurisdictions have made it illegal to leave a dog chained or tied. Even if it's legal, it's no way to treat a best friend.

Still Want Multiple Dogs?

I've lived most of my life with multiple dogs, ranging from Chihuahuas to a Wolfhound and a Deerhound (yes, at the same time!). Life with more than one dog is not for everyone, but it can offer many rewards. If you've considered the cons as well as the pros and decided that you do want more than one furry face in your life, or if they're already there, then please read on.

The Domestic Pack

Chapter 2

Just One More—

Introducing a Newcomer

Getting a new dog, whether he's your second or fourth or whatever, is always exciting. It can also be a bit nerve-racking as you ask yourself if you're making the right choice. Will the new dog fit in? Will the dog or dogs you have now accept him? Will they be jealous or think that you don't love them anymore? Will he be too energetic for your elderly dog? You may even wonder if there's any chance the newcomer will bring in an infectious disease or parasites.

Let's see what you can do to make the transition to one-more-dog status as safe and smooth as possible, beginning with understanding how dogs think and behave.

Understanding the Inner Dog

Most dogs enjoy the company of other dogs. When they live together, they form relationships with one another ranging from obvious love and affection to tolerance or indifference to outright dislike. Watch your dogs interact and you'll see that they use body language, eye contact, vocalization, physical contact, and other methods to express dominance, submission, concern, affection, and love. The richness of the canine emotional life is probably a big reason that human beings have shared home and hearth with dogs for some 10,000 years.

Understand Them for Themselves

On the other hand, dogs aren't little furry people. If we pretend that they are, we rob them of the fine qualities and genetic heritage that make them dogs. We also rob ourselves of the opportunity to understand and love them for themselves, as a distinct species with which we're fortunate enough to share our lives. And on a purely practical level, if you don't try to understand your dogs as dogs, you limit your ability to communicate with and understand them, and that makes

life with dogs more difficult and less fulfilling.

Your dogs aren't just members of your pack—they are also individuals with their own needs, interests, and emotions. Learning to understand at least some aspects of their "inner dogs" isn't only fascinating in its own right, but it's also essential if you want to motivate your dogs to do what you want them to do and avoid behaviors you don't want. Some understanding of each individual may also help you encourage harmony among your dogs. In other words, if you want to live in harmony with multiple dogs, you need to get inside their heads and hearts.

Almost everything your dogs do is based on either learning or instinct, so let's look first at some basic canine instincts.

Understand Their Instincts

Instincts are inborn behaviors or drives that have developed over many generations to support survival. All healthy dogs regardless of breed share certain instincts to some degree, including the instinct to:

- form social bonds (which enables them to bond to other dogs and to us)
- find a "rank" in the group based on individual personality
- chase and kill prey (or flying discs and squeaky toys)
- fight or flee from perceived danger (which can be modified through socialization and training)
- keep their eating and living areas clean (which helps make dogs amenable to potty training)
- mark territory and "read" other dogs' markings
- reproduce (which can be eliminated by spaying or neutering)

Understand Their Genetic Makeup

A breed is a population of animals that, when mated with one another, produces offspring with a predictable set of traits because the genes for those traits are highly concentrated in the breed's population and other genes are absent or rare. All modern (and ancient) dog breeds are the result of selective breeding, the process by which people select and breed animals with specific traits. Selective breeding has produced dog breeds that excel at many jobs: hunting, guarding, controlling livestock, pulling and carrying loads, helping hunters, and simply being wonderful companions. Physical traits, such as size, coat length and texture, colors, and so on, have usually been part of the selection process because those traits helped the dogs do their jobs. So whether they're

If you plan to or do keep more than one dog, it's important that you understand the dog hierarchy and pack behavior.

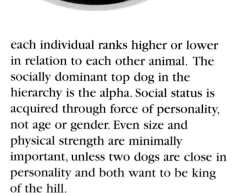

The alpha dog may think that he's in charge, but it's important that you establish yourself as the real top dog.

purebreds or mixtures of various breeds, your dogs' genetic makeups affect not only their physical characteristics but their personalities and behaviors as well.

Of course, individual dogs aren't interchangeable, even if they're members of the same breed. Puppies in a single litter will vary in personalities, physical traits, and talents. But two dogs of the same breed share more traits than either shares with dogs of other breeds, and we can predict at least a tendency to behave in certain ways if we know the individual's breed (or breeds), or more to the point, what the individual dog's ancestors were designed to do.

The more you know about what your dogs' ancestors were bred to do, the better you will understand each one's behaviors, including how they relate to one another. In terms of group dynamics, knowing that one or more of your dogs carry genes that urge him to hunt cooperatively in a pack or to be scrappy with other dogs will help you understand why your dogs interact as they do. That will make it easier to anticipate potential problems and prevent or correct them.

Understand Who's in Charge

Dogs who live together organize themselves into a hierarchy in which each individual ranks higher or lower in relation to each other animal. The socially dominant top dog in the hierarchy is the alpha. Social status is acquired through force of personality, not age or gender. Even size and physical strength are minimally important, unless two dogs are close in personality and both want to be king of the hill.

Alpha Behavior

In a household pack of dogs, the alpha may "own" all of the toys, taking them from the other dogs when he wants to. He sleeps in the "best" dog bed (or the "best" end of the couch until you want it). He's often the first one through doors and gates, and he leads the way on walks. But status in many household packs is fairly fluid. One dog may be more dominant in the house while another takes over outdoors, and relative status may change over time as dogs age or develop health problems. Each individual's position may also change when the group gains or loses a member, including noncanine family members.

Dominance and Submission

Dominance among dogs is established primarily through ritualized behaviors. Knowing something about canine body language and how it's used to assert dominance is essential not only for understanding interactions among your dogs but also as an important tool for communicating your own higher rank to your dogs. These behaviors can be quite subtle, and you may have to observe your dogs carefully for a few days to pick up on some of them. For instance, staring expresses dominance;

averting the eyes expresses submission. Mounting another animal of either sex (outside of mating) expresses dominance; allowing oneself to be mounted shows submission. Placing one or both front paws on another dog's neck or shoulder is a dominant behavior; allowing one's neck or shoulder to be pawed is submissive. Submission is also signaled by lying down, rolling belly up, and urinating.

Let the Hierarchy Be Established

In some breeds, most dogs get along well with other dogs, and differences in rank are established easily and are sometimes so subtle that you may not even notice unless you watch closely. Individuals of other breeds are more prone to contesting one another's status, and members of the same sex

Do your best to recognize and maintain the hierarchy that's established among your dogs, and don't allow one dog to beat up or attack another.

may squabble—yet another reason to learn as much as possible about the breeds with which you live.

As long as your dogs do it without fighting, it's important to let them establish their social rankings themselves. If you expect them to live by human ideals of equality and fairness, or if you try to impose your own idea of which one should be the top dog, you will cause tension in the group, which may lead to fights. On the other hand, you can reinforce harmony among multiple dogs by paying attention to their interactions and respecting their self-imposed hierarchy. Here are some everyday things you can do to support the alpha dog but retain your own status as the ultimate alpha:

- Feed the alpha first, then the other(s) in order of their dominance. (I don't mean let the alpha finish before feeding the others; just offer their food in that order.)

- When you hand out treats, again, alpha first, then the others (in order of rank if possible). If there's only enough for one, give it to the alpha.

- If you buy one new toy, give it to the alpha. If you buy one for each dog, don't interfere if the alpha takes them all. That's his right, and he won't keep them forever. If you continuously take them from him,

you will undermine his authority.

- Give the alpha your attention before the others. He should be the first to be petted, walked, groomed, and so on.

Now, I'm not suggesting that the alpha should hog all of the cookies, toys, and attention. Remember, you and the other people in the family outrank all of the dogs, and even the alpha has to defer to your decisions. Sometimes that means telling the more dominant dog to back off and let the subordinate have the goodies for a bit. But do keep in mind that if you consistently impose your notions of fairness on your dogs, making them take turns or share and share alike, you undermine their own notions of social organization, encourage wannabes to challenge the more dominant animals, and in general create chaos.

Your Status in the Pack

What about *your* status in the pack? The bottom line for a happy life with dogs, whether you have one or several, is this: All the human members of the family must hold higher status in the pack than all of the dogs *from the canine perspective*. You may think that it's cute when the dogs bark at you to get their dinner or a treat. You may think that it's no big deal to sit in a different chair when Fido is curled up in your favorite. But through your dogs' eyes, your behavior looks like deference. And if you defer to your dogs' authority, who do they think is really in charge?

It's usually fairly easy to reassert your status if you've lost it. You don't need to yell or use physical punishment—in fact, those tactics do nothing to create or reinforce a good relationship with your dogs. But you can and should act as a benevolent dictator. Here are a few scenarios to give you the idea.

Are your dogs yapping at you as you get their dinner? Stop all forward motion until they are quiet. Don't shout or get excited. Just ignore them. If necessary, walk out of the room and wait until they're quiet before you go back. They may not catch on immediately, especially if they've been ordering you around for a while, but if you're patient and consistent, they'll figure it out. You can even up the ante by having them all sit or lie down quietly while you fill their bowls. The point is that you bestow your bounty on them because you want to, not because they demand it.

Are your dogs lying in a doorway or all over the kitchen while you cook? Tell them to move, and keep walking into their space. Don't step on anyone or trip, but make them accommodate you.

Are your dogs curled up in your favorite chair or sprawled across

A harmonious house is one where every dog knows his place and plays nicely, one where the dogs respect each other as well as you and your family.

Kids and a New Dog

New dog in the house? Your kids are probably thrilled. But until you really know this newcomer, exercise extra precautions. If your child is old enough to understand, explain that the new dog needs a little time to adjust (just like the child would in a strange place). If your child is too young to understand, a responsible adult needs to be involved directly in all interactions between child and new dog. Be cautious, too, if your other dogs are likely to guard your child against the new dog.

your bed? As alpha, you're entitled to the best seat in the house. Make them move. You can choose to share, of course, but only when you're comfy and only if the dogs defer to you easily. The first time one of them resists your right to that space, he should lose his own right to be there for a few days.

The Hierarchy and Children

Problems sometimes arise when there are children in the family. From the canine perspective, children, especially infants and toddlers, are simply young animals and not at all the same as adult humans. Adolescent dogs in particular may have trouble figuring out that the children outrank them because they're still learning where they themselves fit into the pack hierarchy. Occasionally an adult dog, too, may think that he outranks a child. Any time a dog of any age begins to challenge a child's status, the potential exists for tragic results. Even if your dogs aren't interested in exerting their dominance over a child, there's always the possibility that child and dog may frighten or injure one another. To keep children and dogs safe and secure, follow the suggestions in the sidebar "Safety for Kids and Dogs." (See Chapter 1.)

Dealing With Dog–Dog Conflict

Occasionally, two dogs in a household simply will not get along together. Sometimes they're both vying for the alpha dog position and neither is willing to give up. Sometimes they just don't like one another.

If you can assert enough authority to prevent fights when you're present, and if you can keep the two dogs safely separated when you aren't with them, then you may be able to manage the situation. For many people, though, the need for perpetual surveillance is simply not practical, and it takes the pleasure out of living with multiple dogs. It can also expose both dogs and people to the danger of being bitten if a fight breaks out.

Don't let a conflict between two or more of your dogs escalate. If a problem arises, get professional help quickly. In the meantime, keep the dogs separated, and be careful.

Before You Add to Your Family

The first thing to do before you decide to add an additional dog to your family is to consider carefully the points raised in Chapter 1. If you've done that and you're confident that you have the resources to care for all of your dogs without losing your shirt or your mind, then it's time to get on with the practical matters.

Unless he shows up at your front door or someone offers him to you, you'll have to go looking for your next dog. Responsible breeders, rescue groups, and shelters are all good sources. Wherever he comes from, you'll want to ensure that your new dog is healthy. (See Chapter 7.) Schedule a veterinary examination, preferably within the first day or two. A stray or shelter dog is more likely to bring in a contagious disease or parasites than is a puppy or dog from other sources. Ideally, you should isolate that newcomer from the others until your vet has given the all clear. Realistically, that may not be possible or practical. If your dogs are healthy and properly vaccinated and the new dog appears to be healthy, everyone will probably be fine. If you're in doubt, ask your vet's advice before you bring the new dog into your home.

Puppy-Proof— for Adult Dogs Too

Many things in and around your home can hurt your dogs. (See Chapter 3.) By the same token, a rambunctious canine can damage your favorite possessions and create hazards for himself and others. To make the addition of a new dog go more smoothly, you need to do three main things. The first is to supervise your

A puppy must be introduced to your human and canine packs properly.

Just One More—Introducing a Newcomer

new pooch and confine him to a safe area when you can't watch him. Next, train your new dog beginning the day you bring him home. (See Chapter 6.) Lastly, puppy-proof your home. Here are some steps you can take to puppy-proof, whether your new puppy is seven weeks, seven months, or seven years old:

- Put breakables out of reach.
- Put attractive nuisances away, including tablecloths, runners, cords, shoes, etc.
- Put hazards out of reach. This rule should always be in force, even after your puppies are grown and your adults are settled in.
- Get a list of toxic plants from your veterinarian or county extension agency, and perform a check of your home and yard.
- Protect your dog from chemical hazards.

- Secure electrical, telephone, and computer wires and cables in specially designed sheaths available from hardware and home stores, or use PVC pipe cut to appropriate lengths.
- For a final safety check, get down on your hands and knees and look at things from your dogs' perspective. Ask yourself what would be appealing to you if you were a dog on the prowl.

How long will you have to puppy-proof your home? And how long will you have to restrict your dogs' movements when you can't supervise them? That depends on the individual dog. Some puppies can be trusted by six months of age. Others may not be reliable until they're two or three years old. And older adults who still get into things or who suffer from separation anxiety may be safer and more at ease in their crates when you aren't there throughout their lives.

Puppies and Aggressive Dogs

Be extremely cautious about letting your puppy interact with any adult dog who shows signs of aggressiveness or who hasn't been socialized properly, whether he's your dog or someone else's. If you have a dog you know to be aggressive toward other dogs, don't bring home a puppy (or older dog) unless you know how you will keep him safe. Young puppies, like all babies, are delicate creatures. An aggressive adult can injure or kill a puppy in a heartbeat or cause fear that may last a long, long time.

Introducing a Puppy

Puppies—what's cuter or more fun? Not much. On the other hand, bringing a puppy home is rather like bringing a baby home. He will need extra-special care and training. He may cry, and he'll certainly make some messes. He'll need to learn what you want and how to relate to the rest of the family.

Introducing a Puppy to Older Dogs

Bringing a puppy into a home with other dogs simplifies some things and complicates others. If your older dogs are well behaved and friendly, they will help your puppy learn to be the good dog you want. They'll teach him how to interact properly with other dogs, and they'll serve as role models (although you still need to do the obedience training since your priorities are different from those of your dogs). If they're gentle, tolerant, and playful, the grown-up dogs will help use up a lot of puppy and adolescent energy.

Supervise Interactions

Some older dogs are not all that fond of puppies, with their sharp teeth and lack of canine manners. Even if you're confident that your dog or dogs will accept your puppy, you need to control their first meetings and supervise all of their interactions for at least the first few days, preferably for much longer than that. You may be amazed at the antics your adult dogs put up with, but keep in mind that the peskiness of puppies is relentless. If your older dog appears to be overwhelmed or just plain fed up, give him a break. Even mama dogs need to get away from their puppies sometimes, so it's not fair to expect an adoptive relative to put up with puppy play 24/7. This is especially important during the first weeks because puppies younger than four months haven't mastered the subtleties of canine body language or manners, and so they may not understand warnings from the older dog.

Remember, too, that your puppy

SENIOR DOG TIP

Is a New Dog Fair to Your Canine Senior Citizen?

Many people like to get another dog before their elderly dogs leave them but worry about whether a young whippersnapper will be too hard on the oldster. That really depends on the old dog. If he likes other dogs and is in reasonably good health, a puppy or young adult may rejuvenate him. But if he isn't keen on other dogs or is ill or infirm, he may not be mentally or physically up to sharing you and your home. Only you can decide what is right for you and your old friend. Either way, continue to give him all of the love and attention he deserves, and make sure that he has some private quiet time to rest.

will learn important lessons about how well-socialized dogs interact with one another. In fact, that's one of the best things about raising a puppy with older dogs. People who raise single dogs have to arrange for canine socialization outside their homes. Your puppy should, of course, meet other dogs when he's vaccinated and sturdy

enough, but he has a head start with the dogs in his own new family.

Separate Them When Necessary

A certain amount of growling and even firm but gentle mouthing of an obnoxious puppy by the adult dogs is normal. They have the right to tell the pup to stop pulling their ears, biting their toes, and jumping on their heads, and your puppy has to learn that some behaviors just aren't acceptable in polite company. Keep an eye on things. If your puppy gets really out of hand (which often means that he's tired and needs to go to his crate for a nap) or if your other dogs seem to have had enough, separate them for a bit.

Settling In

Don't be surprised if your new puppy cries during the first few nights in your home. After all, consider what he's going through. He's been taken away from everyone and everything he's known for his entire short life. He probably slept with his siblings, and suddenly they're gone. He's surrounded by strange people and dogs. Just like a human baby, he will cry to get attention and comfort.

One of the challenges of new-puppy crying is figuring out what the crying means. He may flex his lungs because he'd rather be out with you and the other dogs than in his crate. If that's the case, letting him out every time he cries teaches him that he can make you open the crate door on demand. On the other hand, he may need to potty, and you do want him to learn to ask out for that. Another problem is that crying puppies can be shockingly loud, keeping everyone in the house awake. And of course, you're bound to feel sorry for the little guy when he sounds so desperately sad. So what can you do to make the first few nights easier on yourself and your pup? Here are some suggestions:

- If you have the option, bring your new puppy home when no one has to be up early the next day. That way, you won't be quite as upset about losing a little sleep.

- Don't let your puppy sleep all evening before your bedtime—he'll be ready to play when you're ready to sleep. Give him a good play session during the hour or two before bedtime, and take him out to potty (see Chapter 6) just before you put him in his crate for the evening.

- If possible, put your puppy's crate in your bedroom at night. He'll feel much more secure knowing that you and your other dogs are nearby, and he'll probably cry a lot less. Having him close to you will also speed his housetraining because you'll hear him if he stirs or cries to go out during the night.

- If your puppy can't sleep in your bedroom, put an old sweatshirt that you haven't laundered since you last wore it in his crate. Your scent on the shirt will reassure him that you're nearby. A ticking clock or a radio on low may help soothe him as well—put them outside the crate, not inside. If one of your other dogs can sleep in the same room, that will help.

- People always seem to buy their puppies tiny toys, but my husband and I discovered years ago that puppies love to snuggle up with big, soft, stuffed toys. As long as he doesn't rip it up, give your puppy a nice big toy to cuddle while he sleeps. (Be sure that it doesn't have any plastic pieces or ribbons that he might pull off and swallow, and if he chews a hole in the toy so that he can get at the stuffing, stitch it up or replace it.)

- Puppies have to potty more frequently than adult dogs, so if your pup has been asleep for an hour or two and then begins to cry, carry him from his crate to his potty area. (Don't expect him to hold it and walk—he may not have

Whereas puppies will want to meet everyone, older dogs may not be so inclined. Slowly expose your new dog to your family and your other dogs so that he becomes comfortable with everyone at his own pace.

that much control yet.) When he's finished, praise him and put him back to bed.

- If you're sure that he doesn't need to potty, ignore his crying. If he learns that making a racket doesn't win his release, he'll quiet down.

Introducing Adult Dogs

In addition to being social and hierarchical, dogs are territorial. When your dog walks around the perimeter of your yard, urinating every so often, he's marking his territory so that outsiders know not to intrude. Dogs will defend their territories, although some breeds and individuals are much more determined in their defense than others.

If you already have a dog (or more than one), he has an internal map of the pack's territory. Keep in mind that his definition may not match yours. He may think that he owns parts of your neighbors' yards, the street in front of your house, or the park down the road. He may also want to defend this territory against intruders, including your new puppy or dog. However, if you have established yourself as your dog's leader, he should accept your decision to allow the newcomer in.

Facilitating Introductions

In addition to being a strong but benevolent leader, here are some other things you can do to make introductions go more smoothly:

- Introduce each of your current dogs to the newcomer in a neutral location, away from your house, yard, or other places your dog has

What to Do About Unfriendly Meeti...

Initial encounters between dogs don't always go very well. If you've tried introdu...
your new dog to your others on neutral ground and one or both are acting aggres...
don't take any chances by putting them together. Dog fights are fast and violent.
both dogs could be injured, and you could get hurt trying to get them apart. If y...
to take them home before they warm up to one another, keep them apart. Here a...
approaches that may work:

- Crate both dogs where they can see each other. Start with the crates several fe...
  apart, and slowly shorten the distance between them.

- Keep one dog at a time crated while the other is loose in the same room. As lo...
  neither behaves aggressively toward the other, allow the loose dog to approach ...
  crate. After half an hour or so, put the loose dog in his crate and let the other ...

- When the dogs both seem more relaxed about the situation, try again to let the...
  outside the crate. At the first sign of aggression, separate them again.

Usually dogs adjust to one another within a day or two. If not, ask your vet o...
obedience instructor for a referral to a canine behaviorist who is qualified to har...
aggression. Don't take chances. Occasionally, there are dogs who simply will not g...
in which case you may not be able to keep the new dog.

PACK TIP

Dog Rules

To promote harmony among your multiple dogs, remember that they interact by canine, not human, rules. Take the time to know each of your dogs as individuals and to observe how they behave with one another. Do whatever you need to do to prevent and discourage aggression among your dogs, but don't try to impose human notions of fairness or equality. Above all, remember that each dog is unique, and love every one for his own fine canine qualities.

marked as his territory. That way they will be on equal footing. Your dog won't feel bound to defend territory, and your new dog won't be intimidated by territorial scent marks left by your dog. Introduce them one at a time so that the newcomer won't be overwhelmed.

- Keep both dogs on leash at first, with one person per dog holding the leashes. Let the dogs sniff each other. Don't interfere, even if you find their behavior odd or gross. Not allowing them to sniff according to canine protocols will prolong the adjustment period. Talk to them softly, and praise them for friendly behavior.

- If you have them in a safely fenced

area where you can take the leashes off, do so. Leashes can create tension by restricting movement, and as long as the dogs show no aggression and can't take off, they will be able to interact better off leash.

- Whether they are on or off leashes, watch the dogs' body language. A play bow—front end down, fanny in the air, tail wagging—says "Play with me." If they do begin to play, you may hear what sounds like growling, but as long as their body language is friendly, this is a sound of play.

- Hair standing up along a dog's spine, teeth bared, growling, staring, stiff-legged walking, or attempts to mount the other dog are threats. If either dog threatens the other, distract the dogs and put them back on their leashes. Keep them where they can see but not touch each other. Wait a few minutes, then try again. Don't give up right away. Some dogs who start out not liking one another later become friends. (See also sidebar "What to Do About Unfriendly Meetings.")

- When the dogs stop checking each other out—or better yet, play for a while—take them home.

- Remain cautious and vigilant for the first few weeks, especially if you already had two or more dogs or if there's a size difference between the old and new dogs. When you can't supervise, put your dogs in separate areas, or (better) crate them where they can see one another. Don't take a chance on a fight.

Helping Your Dog Adjust

An adult dog will need some time to adjust when moving into a new home. How much time will depend on the dog, where he's coming from, and what your household is like. A well-socialized adult dog may be a bit disoriented at first but, depending on his breed and his individual personality, will probably adjust in a matter of days. My husband and I have brought many adult dogs into our home and have found that they're better on day two (after sleeping a night in their new home) and seem to realize that they are there to stay after about a week. Some dogs may take a little longer.

Dogs who have spent time in shelters are often very stressed. The experience of being abandoned or lost and then locked in a cage in a noisy place is terrifying. These dogs have often experienced big changes in a short period. Some come from homes where they weren't treated well before they went to the shelter. Some have been strays, having to fend for themselves. Some of these guys adjust quickly and seem to forget their pasts as soon as they realize that they'll have regular meals and belly rubs. Others need more time, but with patience and guidance, most come around.

To help your new adult dog adjust, spend time alone with him and with all of your dogs together. Take him through an obedience class—it will help you bond to one another, give you better understanding and control, and

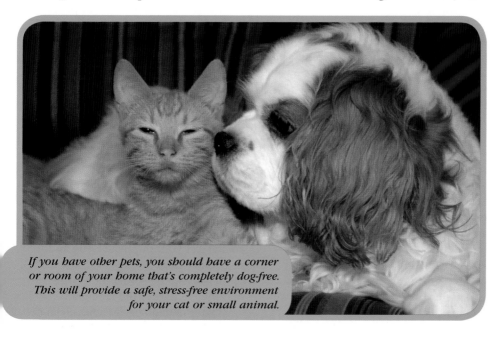

If you have other pets, you should have a corner or room of your home that's completely dog-free. This will provide a safe, stress-free environment for your cat or small animal.

give him more confidence in you and in himself. Give him a crate of his own, and if possible, put it in your bedroom at night or in the room where your other dog or dogs sleep so he feels like part of the pack. Soon you'll all feel like he's always been there.

Two by Two—Adopting More Than One at a Time

Thinking of getting two puppies at once? Sometimes that works out fine, but for many people, it's not the best idea. Most responsible breeders will discourage you, and many won't sell you two at once. Puppies raised together often bond closely to one another, which is fine in itself. However, you have to make a special effort to spend time alone with each puppy so that they will also bond closely to you and the rest of your human family. Separate the puppies for a few hours every day so that they don't develop an unhealthy level of dependence on one another. Both puppies need to learn basic obedience skills, so your training time is at least twice what it would be with one puppy. If you share training duties with someone, the extra

time may not be important. But if one person does all of the training, two at a time can be overwhelming.

If you're adopting adults, two may be a terrific idea, especially if they have been together in the past and like one another's company. Rescue programs and shelters are usually delighted to find an adopter who will take two long-time companions. Even if the dogs haven't been together before, if you adopt two who are friendly to other dogs in general, in most cases they will get along fine. Again, you need to train each one individually, and you must make an effort to give each one some time alone with you, preferably every day at first, so that they bond to you as well as to one another.

Meet the Other Pets

Most dogs can learn to live in peace with all sorts of other critters, and many dogs form fast friendships with cats, rabbits, rodents, and birds. The three most important things to remember when adding a new puppy or dog to a household with small pets are these: caution, caution, caution.

If your new dog is a puppy, introduce him slowly to cats, birds, and other small pets. Keep your puppy on a leash, and be ready to intervene immediately if you need to. Even if he just wants to play, a rambunctious puppy can easily injure or kill a smaller animal. Let your puppy see you and your other dogs interact with the rest of the menagerie so that he realizes that they're part of the family too.

If your new dog is an adult, even if

he has a history of good relations with smaller animals, be very careful until you're sure of him. If you don't know how he might react, keep him on a leash around the other animals until you're confident that he won't hurt them. Again, let him observe you and your other dogs interacting with the other pets.

Never allow any of your dogs to chase or rough up your cat or other pets. Play can turn to tragedy in a flash. Chances are your birds and small furry things live in enclosures most of the time, so they're relatively safe. Just to be sure, keep them out of reach, make sure that all door latches are very secure (some dogs are quite clever at opening latches), and don't allow your dog access to the enclosures without human supervision.

Your cat needs to be allowed to set the boundaries of her relations with your dogs. If she hisses, spits, and bops a pushy dog's nose, don't punish her, don't allow the dog to retaliate or chase her, and don't allow more than one dog to gang up on her. If your cat has been with dogs before and your new dog isn't aggressive, they will adjust. Just be sure that your cat has dog-free places to sleep, eat, play, and use the litter box. And don't take chances—dogs and cats are both equipped to injure one another. If you see any sign of serious aggression or if the dogs play too roughly for the cat, separate them.

With patience, caution, control, and training, your new dog (or dogs) will soon be part of the family. Welcome to life with multiple dogs!

Monitor all play to ensure that all of your dogs are safe.

Chapter 3

The Stuff of

Everyday Life

If you're like most dog lovers, you'll buy your dogs all sorts of toys, beds, chews, and other paraphernalia. Some things are just for fun; other supplies make life easier, and more importantly, keep your dogs safer and healthier. Let's take a look at some of the things you and your dogs will need.

Supplies You'll Need

Baby Gates

Baby gates are useful for confining your dogs to certain indoor areas or for separating them when necessary. Adjustable baby gates that fit typical doorways are available from most discount, hardware, and baby stores. Many pet-supply catalogs offer special gates to accommodate wider door openings, permanent mounting on the doorframe, and so forth.

Beds

Even though your dogs may prefer to snuggle up in your bed, you'll probably want to provide them with beds of their own. Dog beds come in a wide range of styles and prices. Individual dogs have individual preferences, and

your dogs' tastes may vary, so before you buy dog beds, observe where your dogs like to lie down and sleep. Do they snuggle up together or sack out separately? Do they like pillowy softness or the cold, hard floor? (Their choices may vary by season.) Whatever style or styles you choose, be sure that the beds have removable, washable covers. Each dog's bed should be large enough to accommodate his body when he's stretched out and relaxed—or two or more dogs if yours are cuddlers!

Collars and Leashes

Each of your dogs will need his own collar. There are many to choose from, but try to pick nylon, fabric, or leather collars with a buckle or quick-release fastener. Check the fit regularly. You should be able to insert two fingers between the collar and your dog's neck.

You need at least one leash per dog, and it doesn't hurt to have one or two spares. Choose leashes of appropriate size and strength for each individual dog. Some people use special devices called couplers to link two or more dogs onto a single leash. A coupler has a main strap that fastens at one end to the leash, and at the other end, a ring to which two or three additional straps are attached. Each of those straps in turn has a slide bolt at the end away from the main strap so that it can be attached to a collar. If your dogs are well mannered and calm on walks and are of similar size, a coupler may work for you. If one or more of your

If a dog shows possessiveness over a certain item, be it a food bowl or a toy, immediately remove his access to it. If the problem persists and your dog becomes aggressive, seek professional help.

canine charges are more rambunctious on walks, though, a coupler can be a nuisance and potentially dangerous.

Crates

Each of your dogs should have his own crate from puppyhood through old age. Crates make housetraining easier and keep dogs out of trouble until they can be trusted without supervision. If one of your dogs becomes ill or injured, a crate is a safe place for rest and recuperation. If you travel with your dogs, their crates will keep them safe, and if you ever have to evacuate your home, having crates for all of your dogs may save their lives.

You can purchase dog crates from many pet-supply, discount, Internet, and mail-order sources. They come in many styles and prices, so choose crates that will work best for you and for each of your dogs. Most people wouldn't like to be confined to a small space, but dogs are den animals at heart, and most need only enough room in their crates to stand up, turn around, and lie down comfortably. Remember, crates aren't meant to be used for long-term confinement, so your dogs should be in their enclosures for no more than four hours at a time. Check that the crate doors fit well and latch securely so that your dogs can't escape or get a paw or muzzle caught. Some dogs like a nice pad or rug in their crates, but if you have one who likes to chew or rip up bedding, leave the crate bare.

Some dogs tend to be quite territorial about their crates and may

You must prepare your home for your dogs. Certain things in it may seem harmless to you but could seriously injure your dogs.

get nasty with other dogs who try to enter. Of course, if your dogs vary considerably in size, their crates will as well and you won't be able to alternate enclosures. But if your dogs' crates are similar in size, you can discourage possessiveness by alternating who gets which crate. In other words, rather than each dog "owning" a particular crate, all of the crates belong to the pack and you, the pack's real top dog, control who gets which crate at any particular time.

Food and Water Dishes

Each of your dogs needs an individual food bowl. If your dogs occupy the same space, a shared water bowl (or a couple of shared bowls in different locations) should be enough. Your options for dog dishes are practically endless, but they aren't all created equal. Pottery dishes are breakable, and some ceramics made outside the United States contain lead and other toxins that can leach into food and water and slowly poison your dogs. Plastic dishes are lightweight and cheap, but they invite chewing and can harbor bacteria in cracks and scratches; also, some dogs are allergic to plastic. I prefer stainless steel bowls because they're sturdy, chew proof, easy to clean, dishwasher safe, and virtually indestructible.

Toys

Most dogs enjoy playing with toys, and with more than one dog, you'll need to provide enough toys to go around. Dogs don't take personal possession of most toys in the same way people do, but they each may have a favorite.

When you bring home new toys, be sure that there's one for each dog. They may trade toys, and that's okay as long as everyone gets one. You can also provide "new" toys by putting out only a few at a time and storing the others, then rotating them from time to time. Playful games of tug or keep-away over toys are fine, but if the play escalates to quarreling, you need to step in. Occasionally, a particular toy may become a point of contention—if that happens, remove that toy for a while. If it still causes trouble when you give it back later, remove it for good.

Keeping Your Dogs Safe

We think of our homes as safe havens, but unless you have done some serious dog-proofing, there are plenty of hazards for your pooches in your house and yard. Some are obvious—products that are labeled as poisons, for instance. Others are harder to spot.

The Dog-Safe House

The more dogs you have, the greater the chance that they will find trouble. So while it's important to dog-proof your home for a single canine companion, it's even more critical when you have two or more, especially if any of them are puppies or adolescents with lots of energy and little experience or if any are new to your home. Aside from the puppy-proofing steps suggested in Chapter 2, here are some additional things you can do to help keep your dogs safe:

- Keep food containers out of reach, even the empties. Err on the side of caution—some dogs are good at opening cabinets, containers, and garbage cans and at taking things from elevated surfaces like counters and shelves. (A friend of mine had a 15-pound [7-kg] dog who climbed to a fireplace mantle to get something she wanted!) Plastic bags, including those inside boxes, can suffocate a dog. Foil, plastic wrappers, strings, and other packaging materials can injure delicate tissues and cause blockages in the esophagus, stomach, and intestines if swallowed.

- Keep foods out of reach. Your dogs

FAMILY-FRIENDLY TIP

Kids and Dogs, Dogs, Dogs

Dogs can be wonderful childhood friends, and having pets can help children learn many life lessons. But too many dogs and kids together can be chaotic, especially if the adults in the family don't have time to train the dogs (and the kids, for that matter!). Before you add an additional dog to your household, be sure that a responsible adult is prepared to ensure that everyone gets proper care, affection, and education. The adults should model responsible pet care.

don't need the extra calories, and some foods are deadly for dogs. Chocolate, coffee, tea, and some nuts can cause problems ranging from diarrhea and vomiting to seizures to death. Raisins and grapes can cause fatal kidney damage. Raw or leftover meats may contain dangerous bacteria or parasites.

- Keep all medications safely out of reach.

- Keep household cleaners safely locked up.

- Keep toilet lids closed. Toilet water

contains bacteria and/or toxic residue left by toilet bowl cleaners.

- Keep rubber bands, coins, pins, needles, thread, yarn, string, dental floss, fish hooks and fishing line, and other small objects that your dogs could swallow out of reach.

- Holidays pose special dangers to your dogs. Avoid decorating with tinsel, ribbons, and other things your dogs might swallow. Shield electrical cords. Be cautious about decorations, especially glass ornaments that dogs may mistake for balls. Keep food hazards where your dogs can't get them, and keep mistletoe and holly berries out of reach. Be especially cautious when people are coming and going—the last thing you want on a holiday is a lost or injured dog.

Outdoor Hazards

Even if your dogs are confined to your yard, there are some potential dangers. Other animals can be a problem, depending in part on how big your dogs are and how capable they are of defending themselves. Coyotes frequently prey on small dogs and are common in many rural, suburban, and urban areas. In some parts of the country, other predators are problematic, as are poisonous reptiles. Learn about the dangers in your area, and take precautions to protect your dogs.

Many people use a variety of chemicals in their garages and yards, and even if you don't, chances are your neighbors do. Keep cleaners, lawn and garden chemicals, antifreeze, paints, solvents, petroleum products, and other

chemicals where your dogs can't get to them. Thoroughly clean any spills, and if you step in a toxic substance, keep your shoes where your dogs can't get them. Learn what plants are poisonous, and don't plant them where your dogs can get them.

Don't Leave Home Without It

One of the most important things you can do to keep your dogs safe is to be sure that they have up-to-date identification. It may save one or more of your dogs' lives and bring them home to you in any number of situations, from accidental escape to disaster to theft.

Tags

When they're out and about, each of your dogs should wear a collar with his current license and rabies tags and an identification tag with your name, phone number(s), and if you like, your e-mail address. If your dog is registered with one of the national services for lost-and-found pets, include that tag as well. The collar should be a flat buckle or quick-release collar—training collars and head halters should never be left on a dog except during active training.

Unfortunately, even flat collars and dangling tags can be hazardous, and many people remove them at home when their dogs are playing together and when crating their dogs. Collars are also easy for thieves to remove, or in some cases, for your dogs to lose. Permanent identification may help you get a lost dog back and will prove that he is in fact *your* dog.

Microchips

The best form of permanent identification for a dog is a microchip. Microchips are tiny electronic transponders about the size of a

SENIOR DOG TIP

Senior Dogs in the Family Hierarchy

As your dogs age, their position in the family hierarchy may change, especially if you add a younger dog or two over the years. If your senior has held a high rank in the family hierarchy, his loss of vision or hearing, reduced mobility due to arthritis or other causes, and other physical changes may lead younger dogs to nudge him down a notch or two. He may find it more difficult to participate in group activities or to keep up when he does. Rambunctious youngsters may jostle him or knock him around, and you may need to intervene to keep him safe and comfortable. Remember, he still loves you and depends on you. Keep him safe and spend some quality private time with your old dog while you can—you'll both enjoy the time together.

The Stuff of Everyday Life

grain of rice that are injected under the skin over the shoulder blades. Each microchip transmits a unique numerical code, which you must register with a database, that links you to your dog. The microchip is read at close range by a handheld scanning device. Unlike the transponders used by biologists on wild animals, microchips do not transmit a signal that can be located at a distance. However, they do provide permanent identification and proof of ownership.

Your veterinarian can chip your dogs, and many shelters and other organizations offer microchip clinics, sometimes at a reduced cost. If you have microchips inserted into more than one dog at a time, you may be able to get a discount. Some shelters, rescuers, and breeders microchip their dogs before placing them in new homes, in which case you will need to transfer the microchip registration to your name. Even if the breeder or rescuer wants to remain on the registration as a backup, you should give the database your own information.

When you take each dog for his annual veterinary checkup, ask your vet to scan for the microchip to be sure that it's still working. If your contact information changes, don't forget to notify the database registry. It's a good idea to register all of your pets with the same database if possible. For more information, ask your vet or area shelter, or contact the companies directly.

Housekeeping With Multiple Dogs

Living with two or more dogs doesn't have to be a smelly, hairy mess. Here

Spend time with each of your dogs so they all feel loved.

are some tips for keeping a cleaner house with multiple dogs.

- Dogs, including tiny ones, shouldn't potty in the house (unless they're trained to go on paper or in a litter box). If your dogs aren't reliably housetrained, train them. (See Chapter 6.)

- Clean up urine, feces, and vomit using special cleansers designed to remove organic matter (available from pet supply stores or your veterinarian).

- Don't leave dog food sitting out—it smells and attracts vermin (and may make your dogs fat; see Chapter 4).

- Brush all of your dogs several times a week—daily in the spring and fall when they're shedding. (See Chapter 5.) If they require specialized grooming, keep it up to date to prevent matting of their fur and to keep them looking and smelling good.

- Some dogs have oilier skin than others and tend to get a "doggy" odor. Bathe each of your dogs as often as necessary to keep him pleasant to be around.

- Dogs shouldn't have foul breath or nasty-smelling ears. If any of yours does, have your vet check him out. Bad breath often indicates gum disease, infected teeth, and other serious health problems. Nasty smells from ears indicate infections that need to be properly diagnosed and treated.

- Vacuum as frequently as necessary

to keep hair and dander from covering your home. If your dogs lie on the furniture (it's okay—mine do!), wash the slipcovers or clean the upholstery as often as necessary

PACK TIP

Safe Travel With More Than One Dog

Dogs riding loose in a vehicle can interfere with the driver and can be injured or killed in an accident. The safest way for your dogs to travel is in secure individual crates, which provide protection from impact. Second best are canine seat belts (harnesses that fasten to the seat belts), which will keep your dogs from being thrown around in an accident. Either type of restraint will keep your dogs from slipping out an open door and will enable emergency personnel to open your vehicle without having to disable your dogs. If you have air bags, don't let your dogs ride in the front seat, whether loose or restrained. Like small children, they may be injured or killed if the air bags deploy.

When arriving at your destination, teach your kids not to release your dogs from their crates or seat belts until an adult says that it's okay.

The Stuff of Everyday Life

to remove canine skin oils. Wash rugs and the dogs' bedding frequently. Have carpets cleaned as necessary.

- Don't try to mask doggy odors with heavy perfumes—they won't fool anyone but you!

Your Dogs and Your Neighbors

Most people like, or at least tolerate, dogs. Yet dogs cause considerable friction among people. You may have had neighbors who let their dogs potty or dig in your yard, harass you or your pets, or bark for hours at a time.

Preventing these behaviors would seem to be common courtesy, and yet too many dog owners allow their dogs to disturb other people.

If we want to retain our rights to own dogs and spend time with them in our neighborhoods, parks, and elsewhere, we must behave responsibly. And the more dogs we have, the more responsibility we bear to keep them from bothering other people and to set an example that others may (hopefully) follow. There's plenty of bad press about dogs. Here are some ways to get your dogs some positive attention.

- Train your dogs. People appreciate

well-behaved dogs, and your life at home will be more pleasant.

- Don't let your dogs bark too much. Most people won't mind occasional barking, but no one wants to listen to your dogs mouthing off endlessly. Excessive barking may even get you a citation if there's a noise ordinance where you live.

- Pick up your dog's feces and dispose of them properly. Granted, it's not the best part of living with dogs, but if you don't want to deal with it, why should anyone else? Some places have laws requiring owners to clean up after their dogs, but even if it's not the law where you live, be considerate. Feces smell bad, attract insects, and can spread disease. They're not so nice to step in, either. Police your yard daily.

Carry bags with you on walks, clean up after your dogs, and don't let them urinate in people's gardens or on shrubs, flowers, mailboxes, and lawn decor.

- Don't let your dogs run loose, and when you take them to public places, keep them on leashes. Even if they are under complete and reliable voice control (very few dogs are), set an example of responsible ownership for others. And remember, even if your dogs are not aggressive, they can easily meet a dog who is.

Fences may make good neighbors, but so does responsible pet ownership. Don't let your dogs—and mine—take the blame for behavior that is your responsibility.

Chapter 4

Good Eating

The food your dogs eat affects their health and behavior from puppyhood through old age. A healthful diet will go a long way toward keeping your dogs healthy and happy, while a poor diet can contribute to a dry coat and skin, itchiness, hot spots (sores), loose stools, hyperactivity, lack of energy, and other problems.

Knowing how important nutrition is, choosing the right food or foods from among the many commercial and homemade options can be a mind-numbing process, especially if your individual dogs have different nutritional requirements due to age or health concerns. However, if you learn the basics of canine nutrition and pay attention to how your dogs are doing on the food they eat, you can feed them well without breaking the bank or losing your mind.

Nutrients for a Balanced Canine Diet

Like their wild cousins, your dogs are carnivores. Their long canine teeth (fangs) are designed to slash and hold, and their sharp, serrated molars are perfect for shearing off hunks of meat to be swallowed more or less whole. Your dogs' digestive systems process meat efficiently but cannot break down the tough cellulose walls of raw vegetable matter; however, wild carnivores take some nutrition from the partially digested vegetable matter in the stomachs and intestines of prey animals. A properly balanced diet for domesticated carnivores replaces the wild version with cooked vegetables and fruits.

Whether commercial or homemade, a properly balanced canine diet includes the following components to promote good health.

- **Proteins** are highly concentrated in meats, fish, poultry, milk, cheese, yogurt, eggs, soybeans, and dehydrated plant extracts. Dogs need a relatively high-protein diet to maintain good health, but individual needs depend on age, size, activity level, and health status.

- **Carbohydrates**, found in foods from plant sources, provide energy.

- **Dietary fats** from meats, milk, butter, and vegetable oils provide energy, cushion internal organs, insulate against cold, help transport nutrients to the organs, and make food more palatable. Most lower-quality dog foods are high in fat because it's cheaper than protein. Dogs may appear to thrive on such foods for a while, but eventually their health will suffer from a lack of proteins, vitamins, and minerals.

- **Vitamins**, which are chemical compounds from various sources, promote good health in many ways. Light, heat, moisture, and rancidity can destroy vitamins, so food should be stored properly and used before its expiration date.

- **Minerals**, found in various foods, build and strengthen bones and cell tissue and help organs function properly.

- **Water** is vital to sound nutrition. Except during housetraining, your dogs should have access to clean water at all times.

Your dogs themselves are, of course, the real measure of their diet. If they have healthy skin, glossy coats, good flesh without excess fat, and energy and attitude appropriate to their individual breeds and ages, then they are probably eating the right things in the right amounts.

What's for Dinner?

Deciding what to feed your dogs can be tough. If you have three dogs of different ages, do they need three different foods? How do you choose from the plethora of options? For that matter, what are your options?

Commercial Dog Foods

Walk the dog food aisle at any store that carries pet supplies, and you'll find dozens of commercial dog foods. There are foods for puppies, seniors, and everything in between; for fat dogs and active dogs; for dogs with allergies; for big dogs and small dogs. A few companies even claim to have developed special foods for individual breeds. All of these foods come dry, semi-moist, canned, and frozen.

Price

The price tags on commercial dog foods vary wildly, and price can certainly be a factor when you're feeding more than one pooch, especially if they're big. It's important to remember, though, that at least to some extent, you get what you pay for. Cheap foods use cheap ingredients, and many of them contain dyes, fillers, and other things that have been linked to health and behavior problems. A high price, on the other hand, doesn't necessarily indicate the highest quality. Many of the well-known pricey "premium" foods put enormous amounts of money into advertising (that's why they're well known!) but use cheaper ingredients than some of the better, less well-known foods.

Labels

The key to finding a high-quality commercial dog food is to read the label carefully. The first two or three ingredients should preferably be animal proteins, not grains, and ideally, they will be human-grade meats. If any of your dogs shows signs of allergies (particularly itchy feet), avoid foods with corn and wheat—they are frequently linked to canine allergies and digestive problems. In general, the fewer chemical preservatives, dyes, and fillers in the food, the better.

The Cost of Convenience

As the recent tragic deaths from tainted ingredients have taught us, the convenience of commercial dog foods sometimes comes with a price. If you love your dogs, it's worth a little extra

time and effort to research what goes into any dog food you plan to give them. If you're still not comfortable with the commercial options, consider a homemade diet.

Homemade Dog Foods

If you make your dogs' food yourself, you know exactly what they're eating. Let's take a look at the pros and cons of homemade dog foods.

First, you need time to shop for ingredients and space to store them properly; meats, dairy products, and vegetables need refrigerator or freezer space, and other ingredients must be stored in airtight, vermin-proof containers. Whether you feed a raw or a cooked diet or a combination, you need time to prepare the food at least every few days and time to warm it before serving if it's refrigerated. Sanitation and careful handling are vital to food safety for you and your dogs, especially when handling raw meats

· *Kibble (dry food) is probably the most popular and cost-effective commercial dog food.*

No Cooked Bones

Don't feed cooked bones of any kind—they can kill your dogs. Even a small dog can exert a lot of pressure when chewing, and cooked bones shatter into dagger-like shards that can puncture and tear the digestive organs. Keep garbage where your dogs cannot get into it, and remember—as dogs, it's their job to find things to eat, even in the garbage; it's your job to keep your furry friends safe.

that can harbor bacteria and parasites.

If you decide to prepare your dogs' meals yourself, base their diet on reliable information. Good and bad advice on homemade diets is easy to find, especially on the Internet, so be cautious—anyone can post "information," whether they know what they're talking about or not.

Managing Mealtimes

Feeding more than one dog can be challenging, especially if some are faster eaters or pushier than others. Still, there's no reason for mealtimes to be chaotic or overly complicated. Let's see how you can make meals run smoothly.

Free Feeding Versus Scheduled Feeding

If all of your dogs eat the same dry food and none of them have weight or health problems, free feeding may work for you and your canine family. For most dogs, however, scheduled individual meals are better for several reasons, not the least of which is weight control. People often assume that dogs won't overeat if they can free feed, but it just isn't true, especially when there's competition for the available food. Dogs are genetically programmed to eat as much as possible when food is available. For a wild animal who never knows when the next meal will show up, this makes perfect sense. For the domesticated animal with a constant supply of calories, overeating leads to becoming overweight and all of the accompanying health hazards (more on this in a moment). When my dog Jay came to us, he had been free fed and was so fat he couldn't roll over!

Scheduled feedings work best, too, if any of your dogs needs a special diet for health reasons or if you need to include medications or other supplements in a particular dog's food. Scheduled meals are a good idea for other reasons as well. By doling out the food at each meal, you reinforce your status as the dogs' leader and source of everything good, which helps keep order and defuses many problems before they develop. In addition, loss of appetite is often the first sign of a problem that requires veterinary attention. If you free feed, it may be some time before you notice that someone isn't eating. With scheduled meals, you know right away.

Going From Free Feeding to Scheduled Meals

Switching from free feeding to scheduled meals isn't difficult, although your dogs may miss the first meal or two because they think that the food will still be there later. Don't worry—a healthy dog will not suffer from missing a meal once in a while. Naturally, if any of your dogs has a serious health problem, you should consult your vet before making any changes in diet or feeding pattern.

To make the switch, decide how many meals you will give your dogs each day. Two—breakfast and dinner—work well for most people and (once they adjust) most adult dogs. (Puppies, toy breeds, and dogs with health issues may need to eat more often.) Decide also whether you will feed all of your dogs in one place. If you're confident that you can keep them from getting at one another's food, then they can probably all eat loose in the same room. If you're not sure that you can control them or if any are prone to food guarding, then separate them. You might feed them in different rooms, opposite sides of the kitchen, or even in their own crates. However you arrange them, be sure that no one can steal anyone else's dinner—that can lead to squabbles, and if someone succeeds, it defeats the point of controlled portions.

The night before the first day of scheduled feedings, pick up all of the food you have out. The next day at the appointed hour, put the food down for 20 to 30 minutes. At the end of that time, pick it up whether they've eaten or not. At the next mealtime, repeat. Don't give in to begging in between meals! Your dogs are not really starving, no matter what they tell you, and they will soon get the hang of regular meals.

Pudgy Pooches

Are you loving your dogs to death by giving them too much to eat? Obesity, which is epidemic in dogs as in people, contributes to many serious health problems and can shorten your dogs' lives. Most people with overweight

SENIOR DOG TIP

Do Senior Dogs Need Senior Food?

Do your senior dogs (usually defined as seven years or older) need a special senior dog food? Probably not. Research indicates that dogs fed foods marketed for seniors (or other "special formula" foods) are no healthier than those who continue to eat their regular diet. Unless they have medical problems that require special diets, a high-quality maintenance food should provide everything your older dogs need.

Kids Feeding Dogs

In theory, putting kids in charge of pet care sounds like a great way to teach them to be nurturing and responsible. In reality, it's not a good idea. Children lack experience and judgment. If your child is not old enough to take complete care of herself, how can she be expected to take complete care of another living being? A responsible adult needs to take charge of the dogs' food, even if older children help. Here are some ways to keep the process safe and sensible:

- A human adult should always be in a position to intervene when children give food to dogs.

- With more than one dog eating meals, the potential for conflict over food increases. Preventing or breaking up a dog fight is dangerous and difficult even for an experienced adult—a child should never try to break up a dog fight and shouldn't be alone with multiple dogs while they eat.

- Train your dogs to sit and wait politely until the food is set down—especially if a child is feeding them.

- Teach your child never to bother the dogs when they're eating—this includes petting, touching the food, or getting down to food level.

- Teach your child to offer dog treats from an open palm.

- Teach your dog to allow you to take anything away from him, including food. Remember that dogs don't always see children as their superiors in the pack hierarchy, and teach your children never to take food or other things away from your dog even if he has been trained.

- Don't put your dogs' care in children's hands. Pets help children learn to be responsible, but excess pressure about dog-care duties can make a child resent the dog. And it's not fair to let your dogs be hungry, overfed, unexercised, unbrushed, or uncuddled if your child forgets.

dogs either don't see the problem or claim that he only gets a "reasonable" amount of food. Excuses aside, if your dogs are overweight, it's because they eat too much. (In rare cases, a medical problem may be at fault, but that's very unusual.) If your dog eats too much, that's your fault, not his.

Active dogs are more likely than sedentary ones to remain at their proper weights. Unfortunately, most people seriously overestimate how active their dogs really are and how much food they need. People also tend to forget about the treats and extras that their dogs get in addition to meals. That's the canine equivalent to forgetting the candy bar, bag of chips, and iced sugary mocha with whipped cream when adding up your own daily intake. Keep in mind, too, that the difference between 20 and 25 pounds (9 and 11 kg) on a small dog is like the difference between 120 and 150 pounds (54 and 68 kg) on a person.

How to Tell if Your Dog Is Overweight

How can you tell if your dog is too fat? Look down on his back while he's standing. He should have a distinct waist between his ribs and his hips. In most breeds, if you put your thumb and index finger on either side of the spine and move them toward the tail while pressing lightly, you should feel ribs. If in doubt, ask your vet, but be aware that many vets are so used to seeing obese pets and so unused to seeing dogs in proper condition that they often don't mention excess weight in their patients until it's really out of hand. If you're still in doubt, find a canine sporting event in your area and go look at the dogs in competition. (Stick with agility, obedience, or other performance sports where the dogs really are fit—not all dogs shown in

Increasing the amount of exercise they receive is important for combating obesity in dogs.

the conformation ring are in optimum weight or condition.)

Diet Tips

If one or more of your dogs look a bit rotund, don't panic, but do try to take off the excess weight to help them live longer, healthier, happier lives. Here are some doggy diet tips:

- The portions indicated on commercial dog foods are too much for many dogs. Use them as starting points only, and if your dogs gain weight, cut back on the food.

- Measure portions with a standard measuring cup to be sure that your dogs are getting what you think they're getting.

- Don't give in to pleading eyes. Show your love by keeping your dogs at a healthy weight and by training, playing, grooming, petting, and belly rubbing, not by overfeeding.

- If you really think that your dieting dog is still hungry after a meal, you can add bulk without calories to make him feel more full. Supplement his regular food with high-fiber, low-calorie goodies: unsalted green beans (if you use canned beans, rinse them well to remove salt), lettuce or spinach, canned unsweetened pumpkin,

or unsalted, air-popped popcorn (unless your dog is allergic to corn). These also make good low-calorie treats. (I often use green beans or carrot bits for training rewards.)

- Measure out a meal's worth of kibble, divide it in half, and soak one half in water for 15 to 20 minutes so that it expands in bulk. At mealtime, mix the soaked portion with the dry—it will seem like more food.

- A weight-loss or lower-calorie food might help, but many fat dogs stay fat on long-term diets of "light" food. Again, the problem is that they eat too much. Most dogs do better with smaller quantities of high-quality maintenance food and more exercise.

- Limit the treats your dogs get, or set aside part of their daily food

55

allotment to use as treats. Most dogs think that a single piece of plain old dog food is special.

- If your chubby buddy is otherwise healthy, gradually increase his daily exercise.

Age, exercise, general health, and other factors all affect dietary requirements, so each of your dogs will need different amounts of food at different stages of his life. Keep your dogs at normal weights and they will most likely live longer, healthier, happier lives. They'll look a lot better, too.

Picky Eaters

Some dogs are fussier than others about what they'll eat. For some, this is a lifelong behavior and nothing to worry about as long as the dog eats enough to be properly nourished. However, lack of appetite can indicate a health problem (see Chapter 7), so if one of your dogs stops eating, get him a checkup.

If the vet finds that your dog is healthy, there are some things you can

Feeding puppies is different than feeding older dogs. Consult other books or your veterinarian to learn the best feeding regimen for puppies.

PACK TIP

Who Gets What?

If your dogs are reasonably healthy and you choose a high-quality diet, they can probably all eat the same food (although how much each one needs to eat is highly individual). But many people with multiple canine companions feed more than one food because their dogs' individual requirements and health-related restrictions vary. Here are some tips to help ensure that your dogs get the right food, and if relevant, supplements and medications no matter who is dishing up a particular meal:

- Post a list of who gets what near your food storage spot, and update the list whenever changes are made.

- Keep food and supplements together in a secure location that the dogs cannot get to.

- If some items need refrigeration, note that information on your posted list.

- If one or more of your dogs take medications at mealtimes, post that information and the location of the medication.

- If your dogs take different supplements or medications, label the containers with the appropriate dog names. Labels on prescription medicines are often hard to read, so write each dog's name in large red letters on the label to make it easier to grab the correct container.

- Store the dogs' medications and people's medications in different locations.

do to make food more interesting. Your dogs live in a world rich in scent, and their noses make fine distinctions that help them communicate with other dogs, sense danger, navigate, and find food. They live in a world of smells that we can barely imagine. Many dogs who are uninterested in their food perk up if the food becomes more fragrant. This is especially true of older dogs because their senses, including the sense of smell, become less keen as they age.

Moisture and warmth help scent move in the air, so if you feed dry dog food, pour a little warm water or salt-free broth over the serving and let it sit for about five minutes. You can also mix a small amount of canned food into the kibble. If you feed canned food or a homemade diet, you can make it smell better (to your dogs, at least) by warming it slightly. Just be sure that it won't burn your dog—that certainly won't make him relish his dinner!

He Touched My Food!

Food can trigger squabbles, even among dogs who get along well the rest of the time, because control of a vital resource like food indicates rank and power. To control that resource, one dog may try to prevent others from eating their food. Similarly, food may push two dogs who are vying for dominance in other ways to

open conflict. Whatever their source, fights over dinner don't help anyone's digestion.

If you know that mealtime tends to bring on pushy behavior and potential fights, prevention is the best and safest cure. Don't set up a situation that's likely to result in a problem behavior. If you're free feeding your dogs, put them on a meal schedule. If you have sufficient control of your dogs, feed them in different parts of the room, supervise the entire meal, and don't let any dog stray into another's meal territory.

If you don't have that level of control, you need to do two things. First, for immediate problem prevention, separate your dogs physically while they eat, in their crates or in separate rooms. Second, for better long-term control, begin or return to obedience training for all of your dogs. The bottom line is that if you don't control their food and their food-related behavior, then you're not truly your dogs' leader, and that will lead to other behavior issues in your canine family.

Good-quality food in the proper amounts, sensible treats, and a well-planned approach to feeding all work together to promote good health and harmony in your multiple-dog home.

Good Eating

Chapter 5

Looking Good

Regular grooming is an important part of dog care, especially when you have more than one. Some of the benefits of keeping your dogs nicely groomed are self-evident—they look better, and there's less hair to vacuum up. But grooming is important for other reasons, too. Grooming sessions give each of your dogs some private time with you, and they're the perfect time to check each dog for cuts, bites, bumps, sore spots, uninvited passengers like fleas and ticks, and other early signs of health problems, some of which could spread through the whole doggy family if not dealt with early.

The prospect of grooming a number of dogs can be daunting, and it's easy to let it slide in favor of a romp in the yard. Depending on your dogs' needs and how many dogs you have, grooming sessions may be less onerous if you stagger them throughout the week.

Grooming Supplies

The supplies and equipment needed to keep your dogs well groomed depend on how big or small your individual dogs are, what types of coats they have, and whether you plan to do all of their grooming or just maintenance between visits to a professional groomer. Although you can spend a fortune for top-of-the-line tools and supplies, most pet owners can get by with a few basic items. These include brushes, shedding tools, nail clippers, toothbrushes, a mild shampoo, and an ear-cleaning product. Other optional grooming tools can come in handy but aren't really necessary for most dogs, including: a blow-dryer with a cool setting (don't blow hot air on your dogs—you can easily overheat them); eye-care products (ask your vet); scissors, thinning sheers, and/or electric clippers if you want to do your own doggy coiffures; a spray bottle for water and other products; canine coat conditioner and/or detangler; and a grooming table to save your back.

Coat and Skin Care

Healthy coats and skin start with good nutrition, health care, and parasite

Grooming time is the best time to check your dogs for any bumps, scratches, or external parasites that their coats may be hiding.

control. Regular brushing enhances naturally healthy coats and skin by stimulating the sebaceous (oil) glands and distributing the oils for lubrication. Brushing and combing also eliminate tangles in longer coats, preventing mats that can harbor parasites or trap heat and moisture, leading to sores and infections. Regular brushing reduces the amount of hair in your home as well.

Although some dogs don't need to be bathed very often, most do occasionally. Brush each dog thoroughly before his bath. Use a mild shampoo formulated for dogs and lukewarm water. Rinse thoroughly— soap residue can irritate skin. If you have longhaired dogs, comb or brush their coats while still damp. Keep your dogs warm and away from drafts until they're completely dry. You can speed up the drying process with a blow- dryer—use one made for dogs or your own set on cool, never warm.

Nail Care

Letting your dogs' nails grow so long that they hit the ground is like making them wear bad shoes. Ouch! Most dogs need their nails trimmed every two to three weeks, and with more than one set of paws to keep in shape, you probably don't want to pay a groomer or vet for all of those pedicures. Don't let that cause your dogs' nails to become overgrown. If you aren't sure how to trim doggy nails (or how to control reluctant trimmees), ask (or pay) your vet or a groomer to teach you.

Use well-made nail clippers, and

FAMILY-FRIENDLY TIP

Kids Brushing Canines

Dog grooming can be good for kids as well as dogs. Your children can learn a lot about the importance of good hygiene and the responsibilities of owning a pet by helping with grooming the family dogs. As always, an adult should supervise. Children, especially young ones, don't always realize that they're hurting a dog when they pull hair or press a brush into skin. Which grooming tasks a child can do depend on her physical abilities and mental maturity. Young children should never be allowed to clip your dogs' nails or clean your dogs' ears and eyes. Nor should young children be allowed to use scissors or clippers on your dogs—serious injuries can happen in a heartbeat, even when skilled adults use sharp implements around dogs. With safety measures in place, though, your dogs and your kids can all benefit from dog- grooming sessions.

Looking Good

be sure that they are sharp and work properly. (Shoddy or damaged clippers pinch or pull instead of cutting cleanly and painlessly.) Cut the nails short enough to clear the ground, but try not to cut into the quick, the living part of the nail. In light-colored nails, the quick looks pink from the blood vessels inside it, making it easier to avoid. Dark nails are more challenging, but if you cut below the spot where the nail narrows and curves downward, you should miss the quick. After you snip, look at the end of the nail—a black dot near the center indicates that you're close to the quick. If you don't see the black dot, trim a little more and check again. Don't forget the dewclaws, the little toes on the insides of the legs above the front feet, if your dog has them. (They're often removed at birth.)

If you cut too far and draw blood, put a little styptic powder (available from drug stores) or corn starch in the palm of your hand and dip the nail into it to stop the bleeding. Then reassure your dog, and be more careful next time.

Check your dogs' feet regularly for injuries, and remove burrs, stones, and other debris from between the toes or pads. Dogs with long hair between their toes stay cleaner and have better traction with the long hair trimmed. (A few breeds are not supposed to be trimmed at all, so if you plan to show your dog, check before you snip.)

Ear Care

Irritations and infections of the ears are very common in dogs. Allergies, hormonal problems, and excess

Be careful when trimming your dog's nails. Ask a family member to hold a struggling dog.

moisture can all promote abnormal growth of yeast or bacteria in the ear canal. Active dogs also sometimes get water, dirt, plant matter, or other foreign objects that can cause problems in their ears.

Check your dogs' ears at least once a week. The skin inside the ears should be clean and not look red or inflamed, and you shouldn't detect any strong or offensive odors. If your dogs have different types of ears, they may need different care. Drop ears—those in which the fleshy "leather" covers the opening and traps moisture—are more prone to infections than upright ears and may need to be cleaned more frequently.

If one of your dogs scratches, rubs, or shakes his head a lot, holds it tilted, or doesn't want you to touch his ears or head, something is wrong, even if you can't see the problem. Don't ignore ear problems or try to treat them on your own. Ear infections are difficult to diagnose. The wrong treatment won't help and may make things worse, causing your dog to suffer unnecessary pain and potential permanent hearing loss. See your vet for treatment, and ask for advice on proper routine ear care for each dog.

Eye Care

There's nothing sweeter than the loving look in a dog's eyes, and you can do some things to keep your pets' eyes healthy and glowing. If any of your dogs has protruding eyes or if their breeds are prone to particular eye problems, pay special attention to signs

Wait Your Turn

If your dogs are like mine, you may find one or more trying to push in between you and the one you're trying to groom. Everyone always wants all of the attention! One way to stop interference from the rest of the pack is to use a grooming table (or a slip-free mat on a sturdy support) to raise the "groomee" off the ground. Or simply take the dog you're grooming outdoors or to another room to give the two of you some privacy and quality one-on-one time.

of irritation or other trouble.

Some dogs seem to accumulate a lot of gunk at the inner corners of the eyes. This protein-rich discharge can stain light-colored hair, it looks icky, and it can harbor bacteria and lead to infection. To remove discharge, gently wipe it off with a warm, moist towel or tissue.

Redness, swelling, excess tearing, squinting, or pawing at the face can be signs of infection, abrasion, or other problems that can cause permanent damage to the eye. If any of your dogs has those symptoms, call your vet. Many breeds are also prone to inherited eye problems, so do your

Toothpaste for dogs comes in a range of flavors that most canines will enjoy.

homework and know what to watch for. (For more information, visit the CERF website at www.vmdb.org/cerf.html.)

Dental Care

Good dental care is a vital part of a comprehensive health-care program for each of your dogs. Small dogs in particular are prone to dental problems because of their tiny mouths, but all dogs need regular dental care to keep their teeth and gums healthy. Broken or loose teeth, gum disease, abscesses, and decay are not only painful but may contribute to other health problems, including life-threatening damage to the heart and other organs. Poor dental health can also lead to unwanted behaviors, including excessive chewing and dog breath, which is usually preventable.

Ideally, your dogs should have their teeth brushed daily, but once or twice a week will help keep their teeth and gums clean and healthy and alert you to injuries, soreness, or growths in their mouths. Ask your vet to recommend dental-care products for your dogs and show you how to use them correctly. There are specially designed brushes and finger brushes to make the job easier, as well as special toothpastes made for pets. Don't use human toothpaste or baking soda to clean your dogs' teeth—swallowing those products can make them sick.

Your dogs should have dental checkups as part of their regular veterinary exams. Professional tooth cleaning and polishing is often done

periodically with the dog under anesthesia. Most of the time, this is a routine procedure, but anesthesia always carries some risk. Some dogs, particularly sighthounds, very small dogs, very young and elderly dogs, and dogs with certain health conditions, shouldn't be anesthetized unless absolutely necessary and then only with caution. Before you have any of your dogs put under anesthesia, ask about each one's special risk factors and be sure that your vet is using a reversible anesthesia so that she can revive your dog quickly if things don't go well.

Anal Gland Care

Like other predators, each of your dogs has an individual odor produced by anal sacs or glands located on both sides and slightly below the anus. Healthy anal glands produce fluid that is expressed, or emptied, with each bowel movement. It has a distinctive odor, which is why dogs find poop so interesting—every pile tells other dogs "I was here." If the anal glands fail to empty properly, they can become impacted, causing the dog to bite at the area or scoot his rear end along the ground, damaging the delicate tissue around the anus. Impacted anal glands make bowel movements difficult or painful and can lead to infections or abscesses.

Impacted anal glands can often be relieved by manually expressing the fluid. If any of your dogs needs a hand with their glands, your vet or groomer can teach you to express them, or

SENIOR DOG TIP

Grooming the Older Dog

Regular grooming remains important for your dogs' health and cleanliness throughout their lives. Many older dogs love to be gently groomed— when my Rowdy was getting on in years, he would fall asleep while I brushed him. Other older dogs grow to dislike being brushed and combed, possibly because their skin or arthritic joints are more sensitive or because it's no longer easy to stand and be brushed. To maintain a grooming schedule without stressing or hurting your old friend, try shorter, more frequent sessions, focusing on a different area each time and including lots of smooches and tummy rubs in the process. If your old guy has a long or heavy coat, you might also consider having it trimmed to make grooming less arduous.

Looking Good

you can pay to have it done when necessary. A high-fiber diet helps some dogs with chronic anal gland problems, and in severe cases, the anal glands can be surgically removed.

Chapter 6

Behave Yourselves!

Dog training is the process of teaching your dogs to do what you want them to do and to refrain from doing what you don't want them to do. All dogs should receive some training, and when you live with more than one dog, training is crucial.

When you train your dogs and reinforce their training in daily life, you establish yourself as their benevolent leader and source of all good things. Good training, accomplished through positive motivation and reward, doesn't turn dogs into automatons. On the contrary, knowing what you want makes your dogs more secure, and secure individuals get along better.

Training With Multiple Dogs

Training is important for all dogs for a number of reasons. Most obvious is that a dog who follows your instructions is easier to live with. It's tough enough to live with one untrained animal; more than one untrained dog can turn your home life into high-stress chaos.

To make training effective, you need to give each dog some private, individual training time several times a week at first. Such one-on-one sessions help build the bond of trust between you and the dog and help reinforce each dog's awareness of your position as the pack leader. They also minimize the distractions created by the other dogs, allowing the dog in training to focus on the lesson.

Group training time, though, is

Remember to always be patient with your dogs during training. If you become frustrated, so will they!

also important because you want your dogs to obey you when they're together. Dogs observe one another's behavior and learn from one another. You can't expect them to teach each other everything, of course, but a good example can't hurt.

The most productive approach for most commands is to begin training with one dog and one trainer. When each dog understands and obeys that command reasonably well, practice it as a group. Think of the great holiday photos if all of your dogs will sit and stay!

The Importance of Positive Training

There are nearly as many dog training methods as there are dog trainers, and no single method works for every dog. Nevertheless, there is one principle that all effective methods share:

Training is more effective when the learners—your dogs—are motivated to learn because there's something good in it for them.

Whether you use treats, toys, words of praise, or a combination, your dogs will be eager to learn if they're rewarded with things they want. You will no doubt be a happier trainer and owner, too, if you help your dogs enjoy what you're doing together. Harsh punishments—hitting, kicking, leash jerking, and so on—have no place in a healthy human-dog relationship.

Different dogs are motivated by different rewards. Some are extremely motivated by food, while others work for the chance to play with a toy. So your first job as a trainer is to figure out what rewards motivate each of your dogs. You also need to be flexible as you train each dog, realizing that individuals learn at different rates

and have different strengths
and weaknesses.

Basic Training

Basic obedience training should be
a priority for all of your dogs. Ideally,
you'll take each of them through a
basic obedience class, but even ten
minutes a day of one-on-one training
at home will help them learn
the essentials.

Sit

To teach the *sit* command, start with
one dog on leash or confined in a
small space. Hold a small treat in front
of his nose, but don't let him take it.
When he shows interest, slowly raise
the treat just high enough to clear his
head and move it slowly toward his tail.
As his head comes up to follow the
treat, his bottom will descend (unless
you lift the treat too high, in which
case he'll probably jump for it). As
your dog lowers his rear end, say "Sit"
and continue to move the treat slowly
backward. When his butt hits the floor,
praise him and give him the treat while
he's sitting. If he stands up, don't give
the treat. Have him sit again, and give
him the treat. Repeat three or four
times, then quit.

Down

To teach this command, hold a treat in
your hand and slowly lower your hand
under your dog's chin. As his head
follows the treat, he should lie down. If
his fanny stays up, gently guide it down.
As soon as he's all the way down,
praise him and give him the treat.

FAMILY-FRIENDLY TIP

Not Without Warning

Dogs almost never bite "with no
warning." In fact, they usually
give several warnings of increasing
seriousness over the course of
several incidents. The problem
is that many people—especially
children—don't understand or take
seriously canine warning signals.
When a dog's hair stands on end, or
when he stands very erect with his
tail straight up and his legs stiff, or
when he growls and bares his teeth,
he is sending as clear a message
as he knows how. If one or more
of your dogs display this behavior
toward one another, distract them
and separate them for a while.
If they display these behaviors
toward a person, get professional
help immediately. If the person is
a child, don't allow any interaction
between the dog and child until you
know why the behavior occurred
and have a safe way to prevent
recurrences. And if two or more
of your dogs behave aggressively
with one another, don't ever allow a
child to be with the dogs without a
competent adult present.

When he quickly lies down in response to the moving treat, add your command ("Down" or "Lie down"). Give him the treat while he's down, not after he gets up. Slowly increase the length of time he has to stay down before getting the treat—you want him to learn to stay down.

Stay

Stay tells your dogs not to move from whatever place and position they're in until you release them. It takes time and consistency to teach dogs to stay reliably, but it's a very useful command, especially with more than one dog to control.

Have your dog lie down. When he's completely down, tell him to stay. If he starts to get up, put him back in the *down* position. When he has stayed down a few seconds, praise, reward, and release him in that order. Start with very short *stays* and stand close to your dog. Very slowly increase the time until he will stay five minutes with you standing close to him. When your dog is reliable for five minutes with you right there, give him the *down* and *stay* commands, and take one step away from him. Have him stay for 30 seconds, then step back, praise, reward, and release. Build the time up slowly to five minutes. Repeat this process as you increase distance, reducing the length of time and building it back up every time you add distance.

73

Come

A reliable response when you call your dogs is one of the most important things you can teach them. Dogs who come when called aren't only easier to live with, but they're safer as well. This is one command you can teach to more than one dog at a time, but if one of your dogs isn't getting the idea, spend time with him individually and on leash so that you can reinforce the command.

Begin in a very small room or fenced area. Have small, yummy treats with you. You can call your dogs by name, but you may want a group word when calling them all: "Guys, come!" Call only one time in a happy, playful voice. Then do whatever you have to do other than repeating the command

Behave Yourselves!

If you train each of your dogs separately, you'll find that all of them will follow commands well once they are together.

to get your dogs to come to you—act silly, walk or run the other way, crouch down, play with a toy. When your dogs get to you, praise each one and give each one a little treat. Then let them return to what they were doing. Repeat the process two or three times, then quit. Do this several times a day if possible.

If you can't trust your dogs to come when you call, let each one out separately on a leash or long line until you have trained them to obey. If you let them ignore you, they'll learn that they can do as they please. If, on the other hand, they learn that they must come when you call, they will become reliable and you won't be sputtering in the doorway trying to get them to come inside.

Walk Nicely on Leash

All dogs should learn to walk politely on a leash. Begin by teaching each dog to walk by himself. First, be sure that he's wearing a collar that fits him properly. Your leash should be long enough to allow him reasonable freedom of movement but not so long that it's hard for you to manage. If you're training a puppy or if your dog is responsive and submissive to you, try the "no forward progress" response to pulling: If your pup pulls, stop and stand still until the leash goes slack. When it does, praise your pooch and continue walking. If he pulls again, stop. Your walks may be short for a few days, but many dogs realize very quickly that pulling is counterproductive, while polite walking keeps them moving.

Some dogs, though, are much too determined to respond to the passive approach. If standing still doesn't work, grasp your leash with both hands in front of your waist. Don't jerk on the leash—just hold it firmly. When your dog starts to pull in one direction, calmly turn and walk in a different direction. Don't wait for your dog, and don't talk to him until he catches up with you. When he does, praise him and occasionally give him a treat. This puts responsibility on your dog to know where you are and to keep up with you, and most dogs quickly learn to pay attention and not to pull.

Once each of your dogs knows how to walk nicely on leash, you're ready to double up. The excitement of having a buddy along may cause a temporary training relapse. If that happens, take a deep breath, try to keep your leashes untangled, and repeat the methods you used with the dogs individually.

How many dogs can you safely walk at one time? That depends on the dogs and your strength and leash-handling skills. Two dogs with reasonable leash behavior are usually manageable. Professional dog walkers often walk five or more dogs together. You're the only one who can decide which of your dogs you can manage together. Safety—yours and your dogs'—should always take precedence over all other factors. Don't risk anyone's life and limbs just to save a little time.

Housetraining

Whether you live with two dogs or ten, I'm sure you agree that housetraining—teaching them not to potty in the house or to potty in a litter box or on paper—is essential. Sadly, some people just don't take the steps necessary to train their dogs to be reliable, which

75

Behave Yourselves!

Walking nicely on a leash is very important, especially when you have multiple dogs.

Housetraining Tips

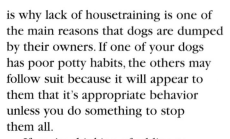

- If you plan to adopt a new puppy or dog, try to find one who has been housed in clean surroundings and has already started potty training.
- Remember that preventing accidents will speed the training process—the less often your dog is wrong, the more often he will be right.
- Be aware that smaller dogs need potty breaks more frequently than larger dogs, especially when they're puppies, because their bladders and bowels are much smaller.
- When you can't supervise your puppy or an adult who's new to your home or not yet reliably trained, put him in his crate with a favorite chew toy.
- Don't expect your dog to hold it for hours on end—puppies need to go out to potty at least every three to four hours, and no dog should be crated on a regular basis for more than four or five hours at a time.
- Even when you're supervising, accidents can happen, so if possible keep your soon-to-be-housetrained puppy or dog in rooms with washable flooring rather than carpets.
- Feed high-quality dry dog food to prevent soft stools and make self-control easier. Allow at least four hours between the last meal and bedtime.
- Until your puppy or dog is reliably potty trained, remove his drinking water two hours before bedtime.
- Regular schedules make for regular potty habits, so try to feed and exercise your dogs at the same time every day, especially while one or more are being potty trained.

is why lack of housetraining is one of the main reasons that dogs are dumped by their owners. If one of your dogs has poor potty habits, the others may follow suit because it will appear to them that it's appropriate behavior unless you do something to stop them all.

If you're thinking of adding to your family of dogs, ideally all of your current dogs will be housetrained before you bring the new pack

member home. If they aren't, you need to put all of your dogs who aren't reliable on a housetraining program or you will have a bigger and bigger mess on your hands because dogs do learn from one another.

Before You Start
Whether your new dog is a puppy or an adult, begin his housetraining the moment you bring him home so that he forms correct habits right from the

start. Most dogs do want to keep their sleeping and play quarters clean, but here are some things to keep in mind.

Limit Space

Your dog's idea of space is different from yours. If he's small, he may think that pottying 10 feet (3 m) from where he sleeps is perfectly acceptable. If you and your dogs spend most of your time in the family room and kitchen, your new dog may not consider the dining room or living room to be part of the living quarters. To help him learn, you need to limit his range to an area small enough that he won't want to soil any of it. For a tiny puppy, that may be only, say, 18 by 18 inches (46 by 46 cm). A bigger puppy may keep a bigger area clean. An adult may be able to respect an entire room.

Give Frequent Breaks

A puppy cannot control his bladder or bowels until he's several months old, and until he can, you are responsible for helping him get it right. He will need to urinate and defecate shortly after he wakes up, during or shortly after each meal, and during or after exercise. Adults tend to develop specific routines, and most need to go after eating, upon waking up, and at other more or less consistent times.

Some puppies can wait an hour between potty breaks; others, especially very tiny puppies, go more often. If your puppy needs to go every ten minutes when he's up and active, then you will have to find a way to enable him to use the right place often. Puppies often last longer when they're sleeping, but you'll have to

Expect accidents to happen when housetraining your dogs. Thoroughly clean up any accidents—if you don't, your dog may go there again.

Crates and Gates

Crates and gates can be your best friend when you live with multiple dogs. Leaving more than two dogs loose together unsupervised is seldom a good idea, especially if one of them is elderly or physically impaired. Dogs in groups sometimes follow very canine rules of behavior, and pack behaviors (rather like mob behaviors in people) can be unpleasant and even dangerous. Unsupervised play can get out of control and result in an injured dog or damaged belongings. Use crates, baby gates, or separate rooms to confine your dogs individually or in compatible pairs when you're absent. But don't use a crate for more than about four hours at a time.

Watch Your New Dog

You must supervise any puppy or dog who is not yet trained whenever he's loose in the house. That means that he should never be out of your sight, and you should always be close enough to intervene and take him to his proper potty area if he indicates that he needs to go.

Your puppy or new dog will eventually learn how to tell you that he needs to go out, but until he does, watch for the signs. If he sniffs around, walks in a circle, or arches his back, he's getting ready to potty.

Be Reasonable

Regardless of your dogs' ages and housetraining status, be reasonable in your expectations. Can they wait eight or nine hours between potty breaks? I don't advocate leaving dogs outdoors when you're not home, but you do need to make some arrangements so that your dogs can relieve themselves at least every four or five hours. If you can't come home to take care of their needs during the day, hire a pet sitter or barter services with a reliable friend or neighbor who can let your dogs out for 20 to 30 minutes.

Be Patient

How long will it take for your dog to become reliable? That depends on several things: his size and breed, his age, his history, and his health. Puppies should show significant progress by the time they're four or five months old, although some aren't able to be reliable until they're a bit older. Adults

make some middle-of-the-night potty runs during the first few weeks. A commonly cited formula says that puppies can wait their age plus one—a four-month-old puppy should be able to wait five hours. But that's a very general guesstimate, and every puppy is different.

Housetraining your dogs will take time, although how much time depends on the individual dog. Be patient!

usually catch on pretty quickly if you're consistent and do what you need to do to prevent accidents. If you have an adult with a history of living in less-than-optimal conditions, it may take a bit longer, but often dogs quickly learn that with a new pack and territory come new rules and procedures. Regardless of your dog's age and background, if housetraining seems to be taking longer than it should or if accidents happen despite your best efforts, speak to your vet and make sure that your dog's progress isn't being hampered by a medical problem.

How to Housetrain

If your puppy acts like he needs to go or if he has just awakened or just eaten, pick him up and carry him to his potty area. Don't expect a young puppy to walk there—he may not be able to hold it that long. An adult or older puppy can probably walk to the potty place. If your other dogs use that area,

all the better—it will smell like the proper potty place to your puppy.

If your puppy or dog doesn't go within ten minutes, put him in his crate for 10 to 15 minutes, then take him to the potty area again. When he does his business, praise him and give him a tiny treat or short play session. Wait a few minutes before you take him back in the house—he may not have finished on the first attempt, and you don't want to teach him to hold it to avoid going back inside.

Housetraining an adult requires the same procedures: a regular schedule, close supervision, and restricted access to parts of the house. Fortunately, if your new dog is six months or older, he should have good muscular control and should be able to walk to the potty place on his own.

Potty Problems

Some breeds, especially the tiny ones, and some individuals take longer to

79

Behave Yourselves!

become reliable. In addition, training may take more time and patience if you have a puppy or older dog who has been eliminating in his own living quarters. This may happen when, for instance, a dog has lived constantly in a kennel run or cage or has been crated so long that he had to potty in his crate.

Some physical conditions can also make housetraining more difficult, so if any of your dogs seem to have unusual difficulty getting the idea, schedule a veterinary exam. Urinary tract infections, intestinal parasites, disease, and even malformations of certain organs can all make control difficult or impossible.

Accidents

Whether you're training a puppy or an adult, expect a few accidents. Your dog cannot learn what not to do unless he makes an occasional mistake. *Do not punish* your dog for an elimination error. If you must scold someone, scold yourself for allowing him more freedom than he could manage. Nose rubbing, hitting, or yelling at your dog will not teach him what you want him to do and may create more problems. Dogs who pee behind couches have learned to hide while they do their business. They haven't learned where they *should* go.

Here's what you need to do when accidents happen:

- If you see your dog start to eliminate in the house, calmly carry or lead him to where he's supposed to go. Wait there until he finishes, and praise him for the part he got right.

- Confine him to a safe place (his crate is perfect) for a few minutes while you clean up. Keep your other dogs away from the booboo as well.

- Clean the spot thoroughly with an odor and stain remover made for organic waste—pet-supply stores and veterinarians carry these products. Remember, even if you cannot detect the odor of urine or feces, your dogs can and may think that this part of the house is now legal.

- Don't allow any of your dogs who are not *completely* reliable to wander the house at will. As the trainee becomes more reliable, allow him into larger areas of the house slowly, and supervise until you're sure of him. Just because he understands that he shouldn't pee

in the kitchen doesn't mean that he knows the hallway is off-limits.

Housetraining Lapses

When you introduce a new dog to your household, be alert for lapses in housetraining among your other dogs. Some dogs react to newcomers by marking everything they consider "theirs," including furniture, walls, and door frames. Some dogs also have accidents out of sheer nervousness, and some may urinate to demonstrate submission to the new dog if he's more dominant than they are. (See Chapter 2.)

If one of your previously trained dogs has a housetraining lapse, try first to figure out what's going on. Ask yourself the following questions.

Is he marking his territory to be sure that the newcomer knows he's the canine in charge? If so, supervise him as you would an untrained dog so that you can catch him in the act. As soon as he acts like he's going to mark something, tell him "No!" Often one reminder that you're actually the one in charge is all it takes, but continue to supervise until you're sure that he's convinced.

Is he demonstrating submission to the new dog? If so, don't punish him—you'll make the problem worse. Encourage the two to play, be sure that they both know that you're the leader, and the tension should lessen in a few days. Until then, restrict the submissive dog to easily cleaned areas when the dogs are together, and clean up thoroughly anywhere he piddles.

Is he peeing on the rug because the new dog did? If so, apply the housetraining routine mentioned in this chapter to both dogs, and clean up accidents thoroughly.

If your dogs aren't spayed and neutered and you have both males and

Behavior Changes in Elderly Dogs

As your dogs age, you may see changes in their behavior. Some of the behaviors we commonly blame on aging can be caused by medical problems that can be treated, so tell your vet about any you see. You can expect, though, that in old age your dogs will sleep longer and more soundly and will tire more easily. They may also become less resilient to jostling and rough play. Be sure your seniors have time away from any young and rowdy dogs you have. Whatever you do, remember that the old guys still love and need you.

females in the house, the introduction of a newcomer may trigger urine marking as part of courtship, especially if the female is in heat.

Problem Behaviors With Multiple Dogs

The more dogs you have, the more potential there is for them to behave in ways that you find objectionable. Let's see what you can do about some of the more common behavioral issues that crop up when dogs live in groups.

Ignoring Commands

Many people have very low expectations about how well their dogs will respond to their commands. The sad thing is that all dogs, from the tiniest toy to the biggest galoot, can be trained to come when called, lie down and stay, not jump up—and anything else that dogs can be taught. It's always more pleasant to live with a dog who has at least some training. When you live with more than one dog, training for each of them is even more important. Training puts you, the human who pays the bills and takes care of them, in charge, and that promotes harmony in the family pack.

So why do dogs ignore commands? Two reasons: They don't understand what's expected, or they have been taught that they don't have to do what they're told. Here are some tips for teaching your dogs to do what you tell them the first time, every time.

- Take the time to teach each dog, individually, exactly what every command means. If your dog doesn't really understand what *down* means, it won't matter how many times or how loudly you yell it—he won't lie down.

- When each dog knows a command, have them practice together—those who respond immediately get a treat. If one of the gang ignores you until he sees the treat, ignore him unless he responds more quickly to the next command. If he doesn't, go back to one-on-one training with him.

- If you don't think that one or more

of your dogs will respond to a command, don't use the command unless you're in a position to enforce it. Every time one of your dogs ignores a command without being corrected, he learns that he doesn't have to do what you say.

The potential for ignoring commands increases with the number of dogs unless you take the time to train each dog individually and then work with them together.

Aggression

When you have more than one dog, you can expect an occasional grumble or even a snap between them. (Who among us hasn't grumbled and snapped at family members on occasion?). As the pack leader, your job is to tell them to knock it off. If you establish your authority through positive, motivational obedience training, control of inter-dog relationships will in most cases be simply an extension of everyday control.

Most dogs can and do learn to live peacefully even if they don't really like each other, but once in a while one or more dogs just won't play or live well with others. If any of your dogs behaves aggressively toward one another or toward you or other human beings, you have a dangerous situation. Don't wait until someone is seriously injured. Get professional help as soon as possible. In the meantime, isolate the aggressor if necessary, but don't let anyone get hurt.

Resource Guarding

Dogs, like people, often attach value to specific objects or places, including toys, food, crates, the corner of the

If you play games like fetch, teach your dogs to give up the toy on your command.

couch, or even a person or whole room. And sometimes that value becomes so important to a dog that he wants no one else to use the object or place. He may growl, snap, or actually attack others who don't honor his claim to ownership. That sort of threatening or aggressive behavior is known as resource guarding, and although people may laugh at dogs who guard resources, it's no laughing matter. Many serious injuries occur to dogs and people when resource guarding gets out of control.

If a toy or chewie becomes so valuable that squabbles start among two or more of your dogs over ownership, remove the object of contention for a while. When your dogs realize that none of them will win and you actually control access to the wonderful thing, they'll usually stop the nonsense. In the rare case that removing the thing temporarily doesn't solve the problem, it needs to disappear for good. And if you know that a certain type of object tends to cause

problems, let your dogs do without.

If any of your dogs is already prone to aggressive resource guarding and especially if any of them has bared his teeth or bitten, get help immediately from a qualified trainer or behaviorist.

Excessive Barking

Barking is a normal, natural behavior for most dogs. It expresses meanings and emotions ranging from joy to warnings to requests to fear. Some breeds and individual dogs are very vocal and will bark at almost any

If you practice commands with your dogs a little bit each day, they will learn to obey when alone and together.

excuse. And when they live in groups, many dogs bark more than any of them would if they were kept singly because they respond to one another and egg each other on.

A little barking isn't a problem for most people, and sometimes barking is desirable—to ask to be let out or to tell you someone's prowling around the yard, for instance. But if your dogs bark often or long, they'll no doubt drive you and your neighbors nuts. They may earn you a nuisance fine and won't help your relations with the people who have to hear them all the time.

The first step toward turning down the volume is to try to figure out when and why your dogs bark and to remove the cause if you can. Do they bark when you leave them outside without you for long periods? Then don't. They'll be safer and probably quieter in the house.

Do your dogs get enough exercise, or are they bored? Even in groups, many dogs are bored and full of energy, and barking is a way to relieve boredom, especially if they can get their buddies to join in. Increasing your dogs' daily exercise with longer walks and games of fetch may help curb excessive barking.

Barking often diminishes as a result of general obedience training. Even if the training doesn't directly address the problem, it improves understanding and communication between you and your dogs and makes them more confident and secure. The time you spend training helps dispel boredom and boost exercise, and less barking is often a pleasant side effect.

Further Reading and Training

For a more comprehensive discussion of these and other behavior issues, please read *Training Your Dog for Life* (T.F.H. Publications, 2008). I also strongly recommend that you take each of your dogs through an obedience class and that you keep up the training throughout their lives. There are no instant fixes or miracle behavior cures. Well-behaved dogs are those whose owners offer them a structured social environment with clear, consistent rules, sufficient physical and mental exercise to keep their bodies and minds healthy, and enough training and motivation to help them be the best dogs they can be.

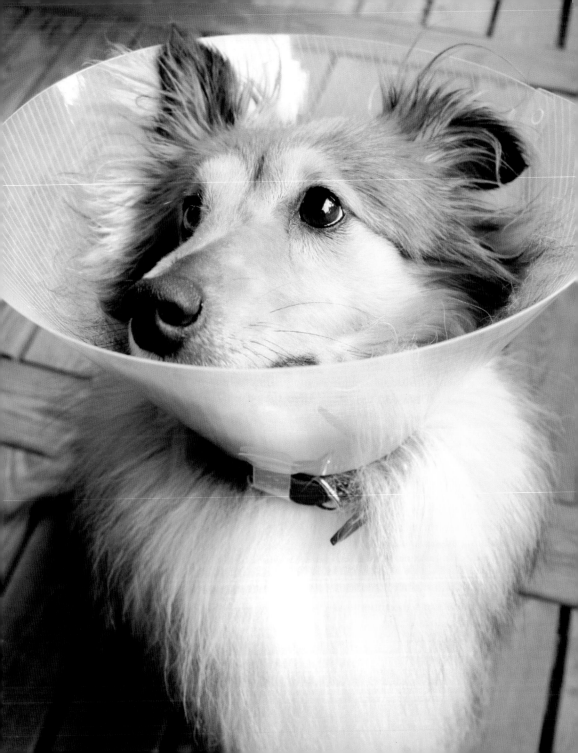

Chapter 7

Feeling Good

In a multiple-dog environment, it's especially
important to prevent the possible spread of
diseases or parasites from one dog to another.
Keeping individuals as healthy as possible and
being aware of their health issues can also help
maintain stable social relations among your dogs.
All in all, good health care can help your dogs
live longer, healthier lives and make them better
companions for you and for each other.

How to Find the Right Veterinarian

It's worth some effort to find the right veterinarian to help you keep your dogs healthy and to treat them when they are not. In fact, you should feel the same level of confidence in your vet that you have in your own physician. Because most veterinarians work in practices with one or more other vets, the climate of the practice is as important as the individual vet you use. If you don't like the way veterinary technicians, assistants, and receptionists treat you or if you lack confidence in their skills, look for a different veterinary practice. You're paying for their services and trusting them with the health and lives of your dogs, so you shouldn't have to stay with a practice that you don't like.

Consider Certain Factors

In addition to the human elements, you may want to consider the following factors when evaluating a veterinary clinic:

- What are its hours?
- What arrangements does it offer for emergency care outside regular hours?
- Can you choose which vet you will see? Can you see someone else if your chosen vet is not available?
- Can you get an appointment on short notice in a serious but nonemergency situation?
- Are you comfortable with its payment and billing policies?
- Does it offer a discount for multiple dogs?
- Does it promote up-to-date

Your veterinarian should love your dogs almost as much as you do. If the vet's office is dirty or you don't feel comfortable with how she treats your pets, seek out another care provider.

vaccination protocols?

- Does it offer or support alternative approaches to prevention and disease?

- Can you drop your dogs off and pick them up later if necessary? Can you see the vet when you pick your dogs up?

- Does the clinic offer other services, such as boarding, training, or grooming?

Ask for Recommendations

To find a good vet or alternative practitioner, contact local shelters, rescue programs, dog breeders, and dog clubs, as well as your own relatives, friends, and neighbors. Ask why people like certain vets, and find out if there's anyone they would avoid and why. The yellow pages or Internet may be helpful, but you should try to visit and meet the vet before you hand your dogs over for treatment.

Routine Preventive Care

Preventive care is essential if your dogs are to live long and healthy lives. If you have more than one dog who all seem healthy, you may be tempted to skip annual checkups to save some money. In the long run, though, you're likely to spend more money treating problems that might have been eliminated or controlled if discovered early on. And where multiple dogs live together, early detection may prevent infectious diseases or parasitic infections from spreading throughout your canine family.

Alternative Veterinary Health Care

Concerns about the negative effects of excessive use of vaccinations and other drugs have led many dog owners and vets to question traditional veterinary practices and to look to alternative, complementary, or holistic approaches to canine health care. Alternative veterinary approaches include chiropractic, acupuncture, homeopathy, herbal therapy, and nutrition. Many dog owners also use practitioners of massage therapy, TTouch, shiatsu, Reiki, and similar therapies. Although they vary in philosophy and practice, a common thread tying these approaches together is the belief that bodily systems work together to affect physical and emotional health. Some alternative practitioners are licensed veterinarians who combine the best of both worlds. Others are well-qualified lay practitioners. But as in any field, not everyone is qualified, so be cautious. Ineffective treatments can delay accurate diagnosis and effective treatment.

Let's take a look at the basic components of canine preventive health care.

Routine Examinations

All of your dogs should have a routine veterinary exam at least once a year to check their:

- teeth and gums for tartar, swelling, or inflammation
- ears for infection or other problems
- eyes for pupil response and retinal appearance
- skin and coat for parasites and other problems
- weight, temperature, respiration, and heart rate
- blood chemistry
- feces for intestinal parasites
- blood for heartworm disease

If your dog needs vaccinations, your vet will give them after the exam, and she will prescribe other medications as needed.

Some owners of multiple dogs prefer to schedule all of their dogs' exams at the same time; others prefer to spread the expense of the exams over the course of the year. Before you decide, ask your vet about a multiple-pet discount and whether you have to bring all of your dogs (or other pets) at the same time to qualify. Whatever you choose, keep track of each dog's records and schedule—I keep a separate file folder for each of my pets, and I use both a wall calendar and my computer calendar to track their visits and to remind me to schedule appointments.

Infectious Diseases and Vaccinations

Concerns have mounted in recent years

Ask your vet if she offers a multiple-pet discount for visits.

Managing Multiple Meds

Keeping track of who is supposed to get how much of what how often can become a real challenge. Here are some tips for keeping doggy meds straight.

- Keep dog medications in one place. (Keep *all* medications where dogs and other pets can't get to them.)
- Prescription labels are often small, so highlight the dog's name or rewrite it big enough to read easily.
- Create a chart and post it near the medications. List each dog, his meds, and the times he should take each. Have everyone who gives medications check off each dose as it's given to prevent overdoses or missed doses.
- Check expiration dates on all of your dogs' medications from time to time. Dispose of out-of-date drugs where pets and children cannot get them.

about health and problem behaviors associated with excessive vaccination. As evidence of the risks has piled up, the American Veterinary Medical Association (AVMA), most veterinary colleges, and many veterinarians and owners have modified their vaccination schedules. Some believe that puppy vaccines provide lifelong protection. Others recommend that after the first year, dogs should be vaccinated on a rotating schedule of some sort. Still others use titers to test for immunity before revaccinating. The exception is the rabies vaccination, which by law is required every year or every three years in most states and many countries. A study is now underway to evaluate the long-term efficacy of rabies vaccines with an eye to less frequent vaccination.

Most canine vaccines are injected subcutaneously (under the skin) or intramuscularly (into the muscle). A few are given in nasal sprays. Core vaccinations protect against diseases to which dogs are commonly exposed, including rabies, distemper, parvovirus, canine infectious hepatitis, and parainfluenza. Noncore vaccinations protect against diseases that are less widespread. Most dogs should receive the core vaccines as puppies. Whether one or more of your dogs should be given a noncore vaccine depends on each dog's age, health status, breed, potential for exposure to the disease, and the type of vaccine.

Vaccination does carry some risk, but it's important to remember that, if used properly, vaccines still offer the best protection against infectious diseases. Some diseases spread very quickly and can devastate a household of dogs. The best way to protect your dogs is to educate yourself about the benefits and risks of vaccination and work with your veterinarian to decide which vaccines to give on what schedule. If you're uncomfortable with one vet's approach, find another vet.

Parasite Control

Parasites are living things that take their nutrition from other living things. Dogs are potential hosts for an assortment of creepy critters, and with two or more dogs in your family, parasites can spread and multiply easily. Don't panic—good preventive care and quick treatment can keep your dogs and your home free of parasites.

Fleas

These bloodsucking insects spread diseases and other parasites, and their bites make some dogs scratch until their skin is raw and infected. And if one of your dogs picks up fleas, you can bet that they'll all soon be scratching as these opportunistic insects hop from one canine host to the next.

Prevention is the best approach to fleas. If you haven't seen any fleas on your pets or in your home or yard,

there's no reason to keep your dogs on a year-round preventive. (Why feed your dogs insecticide if there are no insects to kill?) But if you do see a flea on (or off) one of your dogs, you can be sure that it's not alone. You need to take quick action to prevent a flea population explosion.

To eliminate fleas, you must kill them at all of their life stages—eggs, larvae, and adults. Most over-the-counter flea products are not very effective and some are dangerous, especially when used in combination.

External parasites can spread quickly in a multiple-dog home. The best deterrent is preventive care.

Your veterinarian is your best source for an effective flea eradication program.

Ticks

Ticks are arthropods (relatives of spiders) that inhabit woods, fields, and grass—or carpets, bedding, and upholstery—while waiting for a victim to come along. They then lock their pincher-like mouth parts into the host's flesh and let go willingly only when full of blood. Ticks transmit disease and reproduce like crazy.

If they go outdoors where there are ticks, inspect all your pets daily. If deer ticks are a problem where you live, consider vaccinating your dogs for Lyme disease, which can cripple dogs and people.

If you find a tick, remove it carefully. If it's not attached, pick it up with a tissue and flush it down the toilet. Although you can make the tick loosen its grip by dabbing it with iodine, alcohol, or strong saline solution, there is some evidence that doing so may increase the chances of transmitting Lyme disease from an infected tick to its victim. A tick remover (an inexpensive slotted plastic spoon-like gadget available from some pet-supply stores) makes it very easy to remove a tick without squeezing or decapitating it. You can also use forceps, tweezers, or a tissue. Gently pull straight out (don't

twist). You should see a small hole in the skin. A black spot means that the tick has literally lost its head. Either way, clean the bite with alcohol or iodine and apply an antiseptic. Wash your hands and any tool you used with soap and hot water. Keep an eye on the bite for a few days, especially if you pulled the head off, and call your vet if you see signs of infection.

Mange Mites

Mange refers to several skin conditions caused by different species of tiny arthropods called mites that eat skin debris, hair follicles, and tissue. Mites can cause severe itching, hair loss, and skin flaking and sores that open the way for viral, fungal, or parasitic infections. Dogs are susceptible to two main types of mange:

- **Demodectic mange** often occurs in puppies or in dogs with

compromised immune systems. The mites that cause demodex are present in small numbers on many healthy dogs. Occasionally, they reproduce excessively and cause hair loss. Demodex is self-limiting, meaning that it will run its course in a few weeks and then disappear, and is not highly contagious. It's thought to have a genetic basis, though, and females who have had demodectic mange should not be bred.

- **Sarcoptic mange** (scabies) is caused by a microscopic mite that burrows under the skin to lay eggs. Within three weeks, the eggs hatch and the larvae develop rapidly into adults that soon lay their own eggs. Scabies can cause extensive hair loss, itching, and open sores. It's highly contagious and affects not only dogs but also other animals and people.

If you see unexplained hair loss or skin irritation on one of your dogs, get him to the vet immediately. Don't rely on over-the-counter or home remedies. Treatment is specific to the type of mite, so accurate diagnosis is critical.

Ringworm

Despite its name, ringworm is a highly contagious fungus. It spreads easily among dogs, other pets, and people. Animals with ringworm tend to scratch themselves raw, and secondary infections are common. Ringworm often appears first as a sore-looking bald circle.

Ringworm is hard to treat and harder to cure. Don't waste time and money on over-the-counter or home remedies—they will just delay proper treatment and may make matters worse. Your vet can make an accurate diagnosis, prescribe effective drugs, and help you keep ringworm from spreading through your household.

Intestinal Parasites

Like all living creatures, dogs are vulnerable to several species of

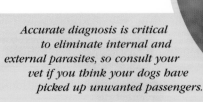

Accurate diagnosis is critical to eliminate internal and external parasites, so consult your vet if you think your dogs have picked up unwanted passengers.

parasitic intestinal worms. If one of your dogs has worms, they probably all do. It's important to know what kind of worm you're dealing with so that you can use safe and effective medication designed to eliminate the specific parasite, so if you find evidence of worms, put a specimen in a plastic bag and take it to your vet. Some worms are hard to spot without a microscope, so even if you don't see symptoms, take a fecal specimen from each of your dogs to your vet at least annually.

The two parasites you're most likely to see are roundworms and tapeworms, which are visible to the naked eye and very common.

Roundworms

Roundworms look like 8-inch (20-cm) strands of spaghetti. They're carried by many kinds of animals and spread easily. Puppies often acquire roundworm larvae from their mothers, even when there's no sign of adult worms in her stool. Roundworms don't attack the host animal directly, but they eat food passing through the digestive system and can cause nausea, vomiting, and diarrhea. A large infestation can cause anemia and malnutrition.

Tapeworms

Tapeworms can grow several feet (m) long. They don't typically show up in feces, although long sections do appear occasionally. The most common indication of tapeworm is the appearance of rice-like worm segments stuck to fur around the host's anus. Tapeworms start life in intermediate

hosts, including fleas, mice, rabbits, and other animals. If your dog eats an infected animal, he ingests tapeworm larvae, which mature in his digestive system. Medications used to kill other worms will *not* eliminate tapeworms.

Other Intestinal Parasites

Several other types of intestinal parasites also affect dogs, including pinworms, whipworms, and others. Some are too small to see without a microscope but can cause weight loss, anemia, respiratory infection, and diarrhea. If one of your dogs has these symptoms, take a fecal specimen to your vet for diagnosis.

95

Feeling Good

What's Normal?

A normal, healthy dog:
- has a body temperature of 99.5° to 102.8°F (37.5° to 39.3°C)
- has a heart rate of 60 to 120 beats per minute
- takes 14 to 22 breaths per minute

Heartworms

Heartworms are long, thin parasitic worms that infest the hearts of dogs, cats, and even people. Mosquitoes transmit microscopic heartworm larvae from infected animals to new victims, where they mature and reproduce in the heart. They damage the cardiovascular system, cause congestive heart failure, and eventually kill the host. Symptoms of heartworm disease range from none to vague unwellness to coughing and other signs of congestive heart failure.

Treatment to remove mature heartworms is very hard on the victim, so prevention and early detection are best. If heartworm occurs where you live, all of your dogs should be checked every year or two, and all of them should take a heartworm preventive regularly.

First Aid

Dogs will be dogs, and when you live with more than one, you'll need some first-aid supplies from time to time. You can purchase a ready-made pet first-aid kit, but it's cheaper to assemble one yourself. Here's what you need:

- 3% hydrogen peroxide (write the purchase date on the label, and discard and replace the bottle once a year)
- antidiarrheal—ask your veterinarian for recommendations
- broad-spectrum antibiotic cream
- directions and telephone numbers for your regular vet and the closest emergency veterinary clinic
- disposable gloves in case you need to handle a contaminated dog
- medicine syringe for administering liquids
- muzzles to fit each of your dogs
- scissors
- small bottle of mild liquid dish detergent to remove contaminants from coat and skin
- small rectal thermometer
- sterile lubricant, such as plain K-Y jelly (*not* petroleum jelly)
- sterile saline eye solution to flush eyes
- telephone number for the National Animal Poison Control Center (NAPCC): 1-888-426-4435
- tweezers
- veterinary first-aid manual—ask your veterinarian or local Red Cross for recommendations

If you think that any of your dogs has been injured or poisoned, contact your vet immediately. She will tell you what you must do to help your furry friend.

A plastic box with a handle and secure closure keeps supplies together and is easy to take along if you travel with your dogs. (You might want to keep a second kit in the car.) Label the box so that it's easy to identify.

There are times when knowing what to do can make the difference between life and death. If you find yourself faced with a canine emergency, protect yourself and other people first (an injured, ill, or frightened dog may hurt you without meaning to, and some emergencies involve external hazards such as traffic), then focus on helping your dog. Try not to panic.

We have room here only for very basic information, so consider buying a good book on veterinary first aid to keep with your first-aid kit, or take a course on pet first aid from your local Red Cross or other source. Now let's survey some common canine emergencies.

Bites and Scratches

Bites, scratches, and other lacerations aren't unusual in multiple-dog families. If a wound is minor, gently clean it with a clean cloth and water. If it bleeds, apply direct pressure with a clean towel, cloth, or gauze pad. *Do not* put hydrogen peroxide on an open wound—it can damage tissue and promote bleeding. When the bleeding stops, apply a broad-spectrum antibiotic. No matter how minor the wound, *call your vet*. Bites and scratches introduce bacteria, and your dog may need additional antibiotics to prevent infection.

Feeling Good

If a wound is deep or long, has foreign matter in it, or won't stop bleeding, seek immediate veterinary attention. Apply pressure to control bleeding and have someone drive you to the vet if possible, or put your dog in a crate to keep him secure. Tape a gauze pad to the wound if necessary, but *do not* apply a tourniquet unless you have first-aid training—you could cause serious, permanent damage. If your other dogs are present, keep them away from the injured animal (a good reason to have individual crates when traveling with dogs).

Bites or scratches from other animals and other puncture wounds that don't bleed retain bacteria that cause infection, so if one of your dogs has been bitten by another animal, talk to your vet. She will probably prescribe an oral antibiotic. If the biter was a wild or stray animal, make sure that your dogs' rabies vaccinations are current, and ask your vet about the risk of rabies or other contagious diseases. Even with antibiotics and vaccinations, infection is possible, so check your injured dog carefully every day for a week or so, and let your vet know if you see any swelling, tenderness, or other signs of infection or illness.

Fractures

Fractures are not uncommon, especially in active, playful dogs and small dogs. Falls, oddball jumps, traumatic blows, bites, body slams, and violent events can all result in broken bones and other injuries. Don't trust the old notion that broken bones can't be walked on—my dog Rowdy barely limped when he broke his leg. Fractures should be treated by a veterinarian as soon as possible to relieve pain and prevent further damage.

If you suspect that one of your

For all of the joy our dogs bring us, we owe it to them to make sure that we can care for them in good times and bad.

dogs has broken a bone, wrap him gently but securely in a blanket or towel, without disturbing the injury. If possible, lift him on a blanket or board to keep the bone stable. Keep him (and yourself!) as calm as possible, and get him to a vet. Treatment will depend on the type and severity of the fracture, its location, and your dog's age and general health.

Poisoning

The world around us holds an astounding number of potentially lethal substances, and no matter how careful you are, one or more of your dogs may be exposed to a poison at some time.

Contact your veterinarian or an emergency clinic immediately if you know or suspect that one of your dogs has been poisoned. *Do not wait* for symptoms to appear—by then, it may be too late. With multiple dogs in your home, it's quite possible that more than one have been exposed to the poison. If you suspect that that's true, take everyone who had access. If possible, take the container or a sample of the substance to the vet, or write down the active ingredients, brand name, manufacturer's name and telephone number, and any antidote information provided on the package.

Sometimes there is no evidence that a pet has gotten into something dangerous until symptoms appear. Although symptoms of poisoning depend on the poison, the dose, the size of the dog, and other factors, they commonly include one or more of the following: vomiting, diarrhea,

loss of appetite, swelling of the tongue and other mouth tissues, excessive salivation, staggering, or seizures.

Depending on the poison, effective treatment may require administration of an antidote, fluids, or other treatments and may require close monitoring for some time.

Disaster Preparedness

Having more than one dog in your home can make their rescue in a crisis more difficult. However, there are things you can do to increase the chances that your dogs and other pets will survive an emergency whether you are there or not.

Post a notice of how many dogs and other pets you have on or near the front and back doors. Stickers for that purpose are available from many vets, shelters, and other sources, or you can make them yourself. If your dogs are crated or confined to specific parts of the house, include that information. Note also the location of leashes, and if

Health Care for Senior Canines

Individuals age differently, and large dogs usually age more quickly than small ones. In general, you can expect to see age-related changes when your dogs are between seven and ten years old. They will begin to slow down and sleep longer and more deeply. Their movements may become stiff, and they may lose weight and muscle mass, giving them a bony feel. Older dogs often lose some or all of their vision and hearing. They often become less tolerant of change, and some seniors suffer from separation anxiety. Don't let your younger dogs overwhelm or injure your old guys with rough play or bullying, and be sure that your older dogs still get regular exercise, grooming, veterinary care, and lots of individual attention.

that your dogs (and other pets) can be dropped at the clinic by someone other than you if necessary. Sign a boarding and medical care authorization form, file one copy with your vet and one with your evacuation kit (more on this in a moment), and give copies to one or two trusted friends or neighbors. If you live in an area that is prone to natural disasters, make backup arrangements for veterinary care and boarding in case the disaster affects your regular vet.

A secure crate for each of your dogs could save their lives, providing a safe way to control and transport them. Make sure, too, that each of your dogs has identification, preferably permanent, and keep it current. (See Chapter 3.)

A clearly identified pet evacuation kit, assembled in a portable waterproof container and stored in an easily accessed place, can provide essential information and supplies in one grab when time is of the essence. Include some or all of the following things in your evacuation kit:

- Important phone numbers. Keep additional copies of the list near your phone, with one or two friends, in your car(s), and where you work.

- Copies of each dog's rabies certificate and other veterinary records.

- Medications, clearly labeled for each dog. Rotate medications once a month with fresh ones. If any of them needs refrigeration, include a prescription from your vet in case

they don't normally wear them in the house, their collars or harnesses.

Arrange safe drop-off sites for your dogs. If a friend or relative is willing to take them, include that information. Make arrangements with your vet so you cannot retrieve the medicine or store it properly during an evacuation.

- Proof of ownership—if someone else rescues your pets, you may need to prove that they are in fact yours—examples are copies of your dogs' license registrations, microchip and/or tattoo numbers, veterinary records, registration certificates, or proof of purchase or adoption.
- A data sheet for each dog, including name, description, sex, age, feeding instructions, health-care needs, and a recent color photo. Update as needed.
- A week's supply of dog food sealed in airtight bags or containers and one or two bottles of water. Rotate food and water once a month with fresh ones.
- Enough cash or travelers' checks to pay for boarding your dogs for at least three days. Cash can be hard to get during a crisis.

Hopefully, you'll never need your evacuation kit, but if you ever do, you'll be glad you have it.

Losing a Family Member

Farewells to even the oldest of dogs come much too soon, and they're the high price we pay for the love and pleasure our dogs share with us while they're here. In the midst of grief, we can find some comfort in knowing that, when the time comes, we can spare them from suffering and give them a dignified end.

The Hardest Decision

When chronic illness, irreparable injury, or old age steal your dog's quality of life so that he seems depressed, withdrawn, or in pain, or if he's no longer interested in the things he used to like, it may be time to discuss euthanasia with your vet. It's never an easy decision, but too much experience with farewells has taught me that if you listen, your dog will nearly always tell you what to do.

Ask your vet to tell you as much as you want to know about the euthanasia process, which is fast and virtually painless. Give each family member a

The loss of a cherished pet affects everyone, including your other dogs. Spend extra time with your furry friends and shower them with love.

chance to say goodbye. It's probably best if very young children are not present for the euthanasia itself, but they should have an opportunity to ask questions and express their feelings. Whether you want to be present is up to you, but if you can, your dog will be more relaxed if he feels you with him at the end. Tell your vet if you or other family members want time alone with your dog after the procedure, and let her know how you want your dog's remains to be handled.

Dealing With Your Loss

Few things in life are more painful than losing a beloved dog. Unfortunately, some people don't understand, and they may say inconsiderate things. Avoid them. Be kind to yourself, and spend time with your other dogs and other pets and with people who understand. Channel your grief in positive ways.

If you or anyone in your human family needs support as you negotiate the grieving process, join a pet-loss support group in your community or on the Internet. There you will find understanding and helpful suggestions.

Sorrow and Your Other Pets

People tend to underestimate what dogs know about death and dying. When I was fastening leash to collar to take Dustin, my elderly dog, to the vet for the last time, his long-time friend Annie came to him and gently licked his face. I know that she was saying farewell. She spent the rest of the day lying quietly on the bed where she often cuddled up with Dustin. I have no doubt that she understood. So don't be surprised if your remaining dogs express their sorrow through depression or behavioral changes when one of their number dies. They will usually work through the grief in a few days and return to normal.

Occasionally, a grieving dog becomes deeply depressed. Symptoms of depression include lethargy, lack of interest in normal activities, or loss of appetite. If one of your dogs shows signs of depression for more than a few days, talk to your vet. A short

course of antidepressant medication may help. And remember, love works both ways—you're comforted by the presence of your remaining dogs, and they're comforted by you. Exercise, playtimes, and cuddles will help all of you heal.

If you still have more than one dog, you may see some changes in the group's dynamics. Territorial patterns (such as who lies where) may shift, relationships may change, and occasional conflicts may arise as the dogs renegotiate each one's social status within the group. These changes will probably be resolved within a few days as everyone adjusts. If not, again, consult your vet, and reinforce obedience training (see Chapter 6) to remind everyone that you're still in charge.

The Continuing Pleasure of Their Company

Eventually, you may want to add a new dog to your family, not to replace the one who went before but to add a new canine presence to your home and heart. Taking in a new dog is, I think, the finest tribute there is to the ones we lose, for it acknowledges the many gifts our dogs give us by being in our lives. In honor of all the dogs of my life, those here now and those who live only in my heart, I wish you many years of canine companionship.

Resources

Associations and Organizations

Breed Clubs

American Kennel Club (AKC)
5580 Centerview Drive
Raleigh, NC 27606
Telephone: (919) 233-9767
Fax: (919) 233-3627
E-mail: info@akc.org
www.akc.org

Canadian Kennel Club (CKC)
89 Skyway Avenue, Suite 100
Etobicoke, Ontario M9W 6R4
Telephone: (416) 675-5511
Fax: (416) 675-6506
E-mail: information@ckc.ca
www.ckc.ca

Federation Cynologique Internationale (FCI)
Secretariat General de la FCI
Place Albert 1er, 13
B – 6530 Thuin
Belqique
www.fci.be

The Kennel Club)
1 Clarges Street
London
W1J 8AB
Telephone: 0870 606 6750
Fax: 0207 518 1058
www.the-kennel-club.org.uk

United Kennel Club (UKC)
100 E. Kilgore Road
Kalamazoo, MI 49002-5584
Telephone: (269) 343-9020
Fax: (269) 343-7037
E-mail: pbickell@ukcdogs.com
www.ukcdogs.com

Pet Sitters

National Association of Professional Pet Sitters
15000 Commerce Parkway, Suite C
Mt. Laurel, New Jersey 08054
Telephone: (856) 439-0324
Fax: (856) 439-0525
E-mail: napps@ahint.com
www.petsitters.org

Pet Sitters International
201 East King Street
King, NC 27021-9161
Telephone: (336) 983-9222
Fax: (336) 983-5266
E-mail: info@petsit.com
www.petsit.com

Rescue Organizations and Animal Welfare Groups

American Humane Association (AHA)
63 Inverness Drive East
Englewood, CO 80112
Telephone: (303) 792-9900
Fax: 792-5333
www.americanhumane.org

American Society for the Prevention of Cruelty to Animals (ASPCA)
424 E. 92nd Street
New York, NY 10128-6804
Telephone: (212) 876-7700
www.aspca.org

Royal Society for the Prevention of Cruelty to Animals (RSPCA)
Telephone: 0870 3335 999
Fax: 0870 7530 284
www.rspca.org.uk

Sports
Canine Freestyle Federation, Inc.
Secretary: Brandy Clymire
E-Mail: secretary@canine-freestyle.org
www.canine-freestyle.org

International Agility Link (IAL)
Global Administrator: Steve Drinkwater
E-mail: yunde@powerup.au
www.agilityclick.com/~ial

North American Dog Agility Council
11522 South Hwy 3
Cataldo, ID 83810
www.nadac.com

North American Flyball Association
1400 West Devon Avenue #512
Chicago, IL 60660
Telephone: 800-318-6312
www.flyball.org

United States Dog Agility Association
P.O. Box 850955
Richardson, TX 75085-0955
Telephone: (972) 487-2200
www.usdaa.com

World Canine Freestyle Organization
P.O. Box 350122
Brooklyn, NY 11235-2525
Telephone: (718) 332-8336
www.worldcaninefreestyle.org

Therapy
Delta Society
875 124th Ave NE, Suite 101
Bellevue, WA 98005
Telephone: (425) 226-7357
Fax: (425) 235-1076
E-mail: info@deltasociety.org
www.deltasociety.org

Therapy Dogs Incorporated
PO Box 5868
Cheyenne, WY 82003
Telephone: (877) 843-7364
E-mail: therdog@sisna.com
www.therapydogs.com

Therapy Dogs International (TDI)
88 Bartley Road
Flanders, NJ 07836

Telephone: (973) 252-9800
Fax: (973) 252-7171
E-mail: tdi@gti.net
www.tdi-dog.org

Training
Association of Pet Dog Trainers (APDT)
150 Executive Center Drive Box 35
Greenville, SC 29615
Telephone: (800) PET-DOGS
Fax: (864) 331-0767
E-mail: information@apdt.com
www.apdt.com

National Association of Dog Obedience Instructors (NADOI)
PMB 369
729 Grapevine Hwy.
Hurst, TX 76054-2085
www.nadoi.org

Veterinary and Health Resources
Academy of Veterinary Homeopathy (AVH)
P.O. Box 9280
Wilmington, DE 19809
Telephone: (866) 652-1590
Fax: (866) 652-1590
E-mail: office@TheAVH.org
www.theavh.org

American Academy of Veterinary Acupuncture (AAVA)
100 Roscommon Drive, Suite 320
Middletown, CT 06457
Telephone: (860) 635-6300
Fax: (860) 635-6400
E-mail: office@aava.orgwww.aava.org

American Animal Hospital Association (AAHA)
P.O. Box 150899
Denver, CO 80215-0899
Telephone: (303) 986-2800
Fax: (303) 986-1700
E-mail: info@aahanet.org
www.aahanet.org/index.cfm

American College of Veterinary Internal Medicine (ACVIM)
1997 Wadsworth Blvd., Suite A
Lakewood, CO 80214-5293
Telephone: (800) 245-9081
Fax: (303) 231-0880
Email: ACVIM@ACVIM.org
www.acvim.org

American College of Veterinary Ophthalmologists (ACVO)
P.O. Box 1311
Meridian, Idaho 83860
Telephone: (208) 466-7624
Fax: (208) 466-7693
E-mail: office@acvo.com
www.acvo.com

American Holistic Veterinary Medical Association (AHVMA)

2218 Old Emmorton Road
Bel Air, MD 21015
Telephone: (410) 569-0795
Fax: (410) 569-2346
E-mail: office@ahvma.org
www.ahvma.org

American Veterinary Medical Association (AVMA)

1931 North Meacham Road – Suite 100
Schaumburg, IL 60173
Telephone: (847) 925-8070
Fax: (847) 925-1329
E-mail: avmainfo@avma.org
www.avma.org

ASPCA Animal Poison Control Center

1717 South Philo Road, Suite 36
Urbana, IL 61802
Telephone: (888) 426-4435
www.aspca.org

British Veterinary Association (BVA)

7 Mansfield Street
London
W1G 9NQ
Telephone: 020 7636 6541
Fax: 020 7436 2970
E-mail: bvahq@bva.co.uk
www.bva.co.uk

Canine Eye Registration Foundation (CERF)

VMDB/CERF
1248 Lynn Hall
625 Harrison St.
Purdue University
West Lafayette, IN 47907-2026
Telephone: (765) 494-8179
E-mail: CERF@vmbd.org
www.vmdb.org

Orthopedic Foundation for Animals (OFA)

2300 NE Nifong Blvd
Columbus, Missouri 65201-3856
Telephone: (573) 442-0418
Fax: (573) 875-5073
Email: ofa@offa.org
www.offa.org

Publications

Books

Anderson, Teoti. *The Super Simple Guide to Housetraining*. TFH Publications, Inc.

Boneham, Sheila Webster. *Rescue Matters*. Alpine.

Boneham, Sheila Webster. *Training Your Dog for Life*. TFH Publications, Inc.

Morgan, Diane. *Good Dogkeeping*. TFH Publications, Inc.

Resources

Magazines

AKC Family Dog
American Kennel Club
260 Madison Avenue
New York, NY 10016
Telephone: (800) 490-5675
E-mail: familydog@akc.org
www.akc.org/pubs/familydog

AKC Gazette
American Kennel Club
260 Madison Avenue
New York, NY 10016
Telephone: (800) 533-7323
E-mail: gazette@akc.org
www.akc.org/pubs/gazette

Dog Fancy
Subscription Department
P.O. Box 53264
Boulder, CO 80322-3264
Telephone: (800) 365-4421
E-mail: barkback@dogfancy.com
www.dogfancy.com

Dogs Monthly
Ascot House
High Street, Ascot,
Berkshire SL5 7JG
United Kingdom
Telephone: 0870 730 8433
Fax: 0870 730 8431
E-mail: admin@rtc-associates.freeserve.
co.uk

www.corsini.co.uk/dogsmonthly

Websites

www.nylabone.com

www.tfh.com

Index

111

Dedication

This book is lovingly dedicated to the pack of my growing-up years—Bambi, Felina, Bonnie, Heather, and Bunti—and to Jay and Lily, the two-pack I live with now.

About the Author

Sheila Webster Boneham, Ph.D., has been surrounded by dogs her entire life. Several of her books have been named best in their categories by the Dog Writers Association of America and the Cat Writers Association. Sheila lives in Indiana with her husband and canine companions. You can visit her online at www.sheilaboneham.com.

Photo Credits